RAISING OTHER PEOPLE'S KIDS

SUCCESSFUL CHILD-REARING IN THE RESTRUCTURED FAMILY

by

Evelyn H. Felker

WILLIAM B. EERDMANS PUBLISHING COMPANY
GRAND RAPIDS, MICHIGAN

For my parents
Olive and Hugh Harrington

Copyright © 1981 by Wm. B. Eerdmans Publishing Co.
255 Jefferson Ave. SE, Grand Rapids, Mich. 49503
Printed in the United States of America

Reprinted, January 1982

Library of Congress Cataloging in Publication Data

Felker, Evelyn H
  Raising other people's kids.

  1. Stepchildren—United States. 2. Children, Adopted—
United States. 3. Foster home care—United States.
  4. Children—Management. I. Title.
HQ777.7.F44   306.8'7   80-28227
ISBN 0-8028-1868-4

The poem "The Birds" is from THE DOUBLE TREE: SELECTED POEMS
1946-1976 by Judith Wright, published by Houghton Mifflin Company.
Copyright © 1978 by Judith Wright. Reprinted by permission.

Growing Parent magazine granted me permission to revise and draw
from material in an article originally published by them: "Planning
for Family Togetherness and Separateness," September 1979.

ACKNOWLEDGEMENTS

It is most important to thank the hundreds of parents who helped write this book, because its ideas are drawn from their experiences with their children. Thanks especially to the women of the Reformed Presbyterian and Blessed Sacrament Churches in West Lafayette, Indiana, and to the members of Tippecanoe County Foster Parent Association in Lafayette, Indiana.

My thanks to Professor Mary Reistroffer of the University of Wisconsin for ideas about the child's relationship with his biological family, and to Professor Rosemarie Carbino of the University of Wisconsin for her early work on the subject of planned visiting.

I appreciate the work of Professor Reistroffer; Claudia Jewett, family therapist in Harvard, Mass.; Dr. Gail Melson of Purdue University; and Wayne Hapner, a foster parent educator from Auburn, Indiana. All of them kindly read early copies of the book and offered their comments.

My husband Don read and re-read the material from first draft to final pages. I gratefully acknowledge his help—as well as the patience and encouragement of our children, who made it possible for the mother of a big family to take time out for the typewriter.

Thanks also to Mary Hietbrink and her co-workers at Eerdmans for their kind and professionally competent help throughout the publication of the manuscript.

CONTENTS

INTRODUCTION

The term "nuclear family" is common to all of us; we often assume that almost every child is part of one. But to a part of this country's child population, "family" does not mean the father, mother, and two children idealized by the writer of commercials. These are the children who have no families, or who cannot live with their families.

Traditionally these children have been welcomed into the homes of older brothers, grandmothers, aunts, cousins, distant relatives—even the homes of total strangers. These people did what they could to help these children become a part of their families. What happened to the adults and children in these families was essentially "their business": if they had more than the usual number of problems or heartaches, hardly anyone knew about them. And the problem child was taken in stride; the family simply breathed a sigh of relief when the child set off on his own—perhaps a little earlier than most of his friends did.

Even today certain things aren't known about homes and families like these. No one really knows, for example, how many children are growing up in homes other than the ones into which they were born, though the Department of Health, Education and Welfare estimates that there are two million such children in the United States. But these children and the families they live in are understood much better than they used to be.

Of course, these families are as individual and unique as the children for whom they are caring. And no one can prescribe a set of rules or make a list of problems and solutions which will neatly solve their every dilemma—just as no such rules can be made for biological families. But many of them do share common strengths and common difficulties, and one family can learn from another's failures and successes. Fortunately, the successes are many: thousands of people have successfully raised children who are not their biological own.

This book is written for all those people who are trying to help a child who is not their biological own grow up well. It is based primarily on the experiences of parents who learned to love, to care for, and to meet the needs of children whose biological parents for some reason could not provide the parenting they needed.

This book is also for families headed by a biological parent and a step-parent. Even though there are many such families, child-rearing literature does not take much notice of their special needs.

I also designed this book to help the growing number of families who have adopted a child to provide him with legal and other advantages and who are also maintaining and encouraging contact with the child's biological family. I have, in fact, addressed a few sections to the biological parent.

Although I am usually addressing adoptive parents and foster parents, I am also writing for school personnel, neighborhood workers, church workers, counselors, and others who are attempting to help families—especially families like those described above.

I will refer to these as "restructured" or "functional" families, because these parents and children are tied together by new familial structures and by the functions they serve in each other's lives, regardless of the presence or absence of biological or legal ties. Both the children and the parents in these families are subject to particular stresses, and vulnerable to cultural myths and other societal pressures. It is important to recognize these special problems so that they can be solved before crises develop.

A number of myths about the restructured family need dispelling. Many people believe them—in fact, if you are part of a restructured family that believes them, your task will be just that much more difficult.

The most widespread of these myths is probably that biological families are more successful than restructured families. We have very little hard evidence that this is either true or false. But if a child for one reason or another appears to be having difficulty in the school or community, the make-up of his family probably will be scrutinized. If it happens that he is living with an aunt, a step-parent, foster parents, or his grandmother, that will probably be considered the cause of his difficulty. Possibly it is—but it is equally possible that the child's problem has a completely unrelated cause, the kind that would be discovered and explored if he were living with his biological family. A restructured family I know had great difficulty convincing school personnel to arrange hearing tests for their new child. His behavior problems were readily attributed to "adjustment difficulties" in his new family. In fact, this was always the assessment—so for eight years the child had been struggling in this and other homes with undiagnosed hearing loss. Of course restructured families have problems which may trigger misbehavior in their children, but so do other families. The idea that living in a restructured family is reason enough to explain such difficulties is neither true nor fair.

Another myth that adds to the difficulties of restructured families is that if one family member has problems, the entire family no doubt has problems. Family counselors often operate by this theory—in fact, they sometimes carry it one step further to the "scapegoat theory." In its simplest form the theory proposes that the disturbed child is not really the root of the family problem but a victim of the family instead: the family blames the innocent child for its problems because it can't handle stress properly.

I'm sure this theory has merit, and has provided a useful framework for helping many families. But its emphasis on current functioning of the family tends to obscure the fact that the child may have developed problems before he joined that family. What the family therapist or other counselor sees may be the family's attempt to adapt to some rather bizarre behavior of its new member. The family might need help— but the child probably also needs the therapist's help to change the negative behavior patterns he has previously learned. Distinguishing between the family's problems and the child's problems may be difficult—but it is difficult for the functional family, too, and they will appreciate a counselor who at least tries to help the child change instead of working only to change them.

Another myth is that biological ties between parent and child are more "real" than functional ones. A legal, social, emotional, physical process creates the strongest bond in our society—the tie between a truly married husband and wife. All of us recognize the depth and genuineness of what began as a meeting of two strangers and grew into this special relationship. The process of creating a functional family requires a similar mix of legal, social, emotional, and physical factors. In both of these relationships a biological bond—like that between adult and older parent, between parent and child—does not exist. But this fact does not make these relationships any less genuine, any less "real." The close relationship between a foster parent and child is just as "real" as that between any biological parent and child.

That is why in this book I will not use the expression "real parent." Reality has to do with what is—if you are performing the functions of a parent, you are a child's "real parent." The child needs a loving adult who will fill a parental role; accept that role yourself, and you will help your child accept it, too. Together you will become a functional family.

BIRDS

Whatever the bird is, is perfect in the bird.
Weapons kestrel hard as a blade's curve,
thrush round as a mother or a full drop of water
fruit-green parrot wise in his shrieking swerve—
all are what bird is and do not reach beyond bird.

Whatever the bird does is right for the bird to do—
cruel kestrel dividing in his hunger the sky,
thrush in the trembling dew beginning to sing,
parrot clinging and quarrelling and veiling his queer eye—
all these as birds are and good for birds to do.

But I am torn and beleaguered by my own people.
The blood that feeds my heart is the blood they gave me,
and my heart is the house where they gather and fight for
    dominion—
all different, all with a wish and a will to save me,
to turn me into the ways of other people.

If I could leave their battleground for the forest of a bird
I could melt the past, the present and the future in one
and find the words that lie behind all these languages.
Then I could fuse my passions into one clear stone
and be simple to myself as the bird is to the bird.

by Judith Wright

CHAPTER **1**

BRINGING YOUR NEW CHILD INTO YOUR FAMILY

Preparing Yourself and the Child

Children are added to a new family by processes almost as varied and unique as the children themselves. Perhaps your new son joined your family as a short-term boarder and stayed on when his family's problems grew worse instead of better. You may be raising your sister's children because a tragic accident took her life suddenly. Or perhaps you were able to make long-range plans and carefully arrange visits before the child came to live with you. Regardless of the history of your situation, some general patterns exist which can help you successfully integrate this new member into your family. I am going to assume that your child has not yet come to live with you, so I'll begin by discussing the planning stage. If your child is already living with you, perhaps this information will help you sort out what has been happening in your family. You may want to retrace some of your steps or try to modify your present situation.

You might think that an unqualified willingness to love and accept the child would be all that is needed for welcoming him into a family. But this kind of thinking ignores the complexity of this event. In fact, if *both* the child and the family are not prepared for this major change, it can be difficult to make. Fortunately, you can take steps to make the transition easier.

Talk about it. All the people affected, even very young children, should be involved in the decision which is going to change their home life in a significant way. I am not suggesting that children must have veto power. Certainly it is the responsibility of adults to make the best possible plans for

3

themselves and their children, and children do not always
have the ability to judge which plan is best. (Neither do adults,
of course.) However, children can and should be involved in
the planning which adults are doing. Perhaps your family can
choose a boy or a girl, an older or a younger child. Let your
children participate in the discussion about this choice. Also
discuss with them practical questions like "Where will he
sleep?" or "What do you think will make a new child feel welcome?" To think that leaving them out of these plans "pro-
tects" them is a false assumption. People who work with
children are convinced that they generally have a fairly accurate idea of what is going on in a household anyway—
regardless of what they are told. And when they don't clearly
understand a situation—the anticipated arrival of a new
brother or sister, for example—they are likely to worry about
what they *don't* know; they are less likely to worry if the situation is clearly explained to them.

Adults should be open with each other, too. Perhaps you
will be raising a teen-age girl who has braces on her teeth. If
her biological father volunteers to pay for the remaining visits
to the orthodontist, clarify this financial arrangement. Financial details like these—and other details like visiting arrangements—can be much more easily handled in the planning
stage. Inattention to such details frequently causes uncertainty and unpleasantness later.

Learn all you can about the child's history. In the past the
strength of a couple's desire for a child was judged by their
willingness to accept him in blind faith, with little or no knowledge of his past. Their attitude said, "His past is his own—the
future will be ours together." Many of these arrangements
have worked out very well, but they can cause a child unnecessary pain. Adults may succeed in convincing themselves
that the child has no past, but the child knows he has. If it was
painful, he needs help in learning to live with the past in the
new context of a warm, supportive family. But even if the past
was not painful, the child needs help to cope with it as he
makes the transition from the known to the unknown. Just
imagine that you are the child, and respond to the experience
as he might.

You go to bed one night in a familiar place with familiar people. The walls of the room are blue, and favorite pictures hang on the wall. There is a window through which you can watch the moon come up. Your sister is already asleep in a crib in the corner. You follow your usual routine—take a bubble bath, skip brushing your teeth again, give your Dad a big good-night hug. Mom has been gone quite a while now, so you have learned to put yourself to bed, but you take along that old Snoopy dog you have had for years. The bed smells familiar and your pillow has all the right lumps. Your dog barks outside as someone passes on the sidewalk, you can hear the people upstairs walk around, the TV sounds faint and far away. . . . The next thing you know it's morning.

The next day a lady comes and gathers up your clothes, explaining that today is moving day. Dad says he'll be by to see you soon, and you go to a new home out in the country. It seems far away but you aren't sure. The day goes by in a blur, and suddenly it's time to go to bed again. A strange lady stands over you and insists you brush your teeth, and says they take showers—not bubble baths—in the *morning* at their house. Then she takes you to a room where you are going to sleep by yourself and tucks you into bed. She is very nice and cheerful, but you can't help missing your hug from Dad. This bed feels cool and kind of hard, and the pillow has strange lumps in it. A girl at the house gave you her teddy bear to take to bed, but it isn't like having Snoopy. You aren't sure what color the room is, and the tree outside the window makes funny patterns on the walls. No, not funny exactly—they seem kind of scary. You can't see the moon. There's something making noises outside the window, but you don't know what it is. The house seems very big and very strange, like it doesn't know you at all.

Though imaginary, this scene shows how an abrupt move from the familiar to the unfamiliar can hurt and disorient a child. Because you are kind and loving people, and because he is resilient, he will recover, but the hurt is often unnecessary. You can help prevent it by learning about the positive details and helpful routines of his old life and transferring them to his new life. Does he have a favorite toy that he should be sure to bring with him? Is there a particular bedtime routine that he feels most comfortable with? Talk with him, too, about the differences he will notice. Explain the unfamiliar sounds he might hear in the night; discuss the color of the bedroom. With a concrete knowledge of his past, you can help him make an easier transition to the present.

His history also includes people he knows, teachers he has liked, books he has read, places he has visited. If you know about them you can talk with him about them, and that will help him handle his very real grief over losing touch with some of them. If you don't learn about these things, you might not know how to respond when your child does mention them—particularly if his stories seem a little farfetched. Is he fantasizing? Is he telling tall tales to impress you? Particularly if his previous experiences were negative, he may have developed the habit of running away from reality by stretching the truth or by inventing people and occurrences. You want to help him realize that he can be comfortable with the truth now—but you don't want to correct him if in fact he did have that rather unusual experience he's relating. Learning about a child ahead of time can help prevent quandaries like this.

You will never know all you wish you knew, but take the opportunity to learn what you can. As your child becomes more comfortable with you, the past will fade just as it does for any of us, but in the early weeks of adjustment it will help if you can act on the basis of information, not hunches. Remember, too, that to some extent you will *always* act on the basis of what you know about the child's past. If that past is a total blank to you, both you and the child will miss it. Charlotte Armstrong makes this point in her book *A Little Less Than Kind*, when the father muses about his troubled stepson:

> How little he knew about his stepson. Whether the boy had ever been to church in his life, for instance. To his own children, he had so many clues. The experiences they'd had, their training, the questions they had asked and at least some of the answers they'd been given, the whole matrix of their adult minds. But to this boy, no clues. Except an old acquaintance with his parents and a great gap in that—all the years of the boy.
>
> Even if a child is older and has consistently blocked out his

past, it is possible to "retrieve" this lost time. Quite recently, professional counselors have been using what they call a scrapbook to help the older child reconstruct his past. They skillfully help the child to remember and record the significant events of his life in a way that makes them more accessible to him and lets him discuss memories that are painful or puzzling. If you are considering raising a child who does not seem to know much about his past, you might want to discuss such a procedure with a local child guidance counselor or a mental health worker. I am not advocating poking around in a child's past to dredge up traumatic experiences or to stir up old emotional debris. But I do believe that coming to terms with the past is a lifelong task which frees us to live more contentedly in the present and to plan more effectively for the future. If you are raising a child who to you is a child without a past and all is going well, I'm glad. It can be done, of course. But I'm convinced that a child whose past is hidden is working under a handicap as he tries to understand who he is and where he belongs.

Visit the child and let him visit you. In some situations a child must be moved immediately from one home to another, but this kind of move should not be a first choice. Ideally, the child should have time to get acquainted with you, with his new surroundings, with the concrete reality of the change that is ahead of him. Because this period of transition between old home and new may be very difficult, a child is often upset by "getting to know you" visits. His distressed behavior and the emotional stress the adults feel may tempt the adults to hurry the move. But some distress to both child and adults should be expected; it shouldn't prompt a change in the moving process.

Even if the first visit appears to go very well, the visiting plan shouldn't be cut short—the child still needs the time to absorb what is happening. Keep in mind that many children, especially those who have moved frequently in the past, may enter a new home with deceptive ease. Experienced foster parents are wary of such "easy moves." They know that a brief honeymoon may be followed by very difficult days when the child's behavior is disturbed. A less abrupt move may not

this behavior, but it at least gives the child a chance
in greater control of what is happening to him and less
the mercy of adults he hardly knows or understands.
Visiting periods, of course, are perfect times to talk with your
child and learn about his personal history.

Do some reading. When you know the age of the child
who will be joining your family, take the opportunity to get
acquainted with the developmental characteristics of a child
that age. (The chapter on developmental goals in this book can
be a starting point.) If you aren't currently raising another
child of about that same age, you may have forgotten—or
might not know—what is considered "normal" development
and behavior for a child that age. If, for example, you're raising children who are four and six and quite suddenly you are
to become parents of an eleven-year-old, you'll need to learn
about eleven-year-olds in general to know what to expect of
your new child.

Use as a guide your own childhood and that of your
brothers and sisters or cousins. It is very easy to gloss over
our own childhoods—to remember only the pleasant parts, to
telescope years of growing up into a very short period in
memory. But make a serious effort to remember what you
were like at your child's age: what you enjoyed, what bugged
you about adults, the kind of scrapes you got into, the books
you read, the worries you had. Such a thoughtful re-evaluation of your own childhood is one of the best clues you can use
to understand your child and to help him grow up well.

Coping with the Changes

Another idea which can help you adapt to the presence of a
new family member is the realization that you are facing a
change—and that most people do not like change. Even when
things are going very poorly, we often prefer to stay in the rut
to which we are accustomed. As Hamlet claimed: "Better to
bear the ills we know than fly to those we know not of." If our
present situation is very comfortable, we are still more likely
to resist change and find it uncomfortable. The first theory
helps explain why even the child who has lived in the most

miserable circumstances may strongly resist settling into the more pleasant routines of a new home. The second theory helps explain why a family currently comfortable and happy may resist making the changes that will help the new child fit into the family circle. Fortunately, you can keep these theories from ruling your particular situation.

First of all, everyone involved should be aware that any change brings stress. It follows, then, that every time a member of the family leaves or a new member is added, the family feels stress and accompanying distress. We are quite aware of this in some situations. The pressure of a first baby's presence on the married couple is well-known. Family counselors speak of the "empty nest syndrome" to describe the stressful situation which may arise when the last child leaves home. And it's common knowledge that parents have longed for the return of the child away at college, then sighed with relief when the child went back to school, because trying to "fit him in" again for a summer caused so much turmoil.

Less often recognized is the fact that the child joining the family may become the scapegoat when other additions or subtractions of family members generate stress. Foster care workers are particularly careful to give extra help and support to a family, for instance, when an older child leaves home, or a new baby is born. They realize that the tension generated by the change might be directed at the child joining the family even though he isn't the cause of it. Simply recognizing that any change in the number of family members creates strain can help a family pinpoint the source of its difficulty and avoid allowing that strain to affect all relationships.

It also helps to be aware that adding a member to the family makes the family as a whole something different. Families are not made up of interchangeable parts or merely a number of persons; a family of five is more than quantitatively different from a family of six. Family members are much like organs of the human body—each plays a particular role and helps make the family complete. When another member is added, the family doesn't just become bigger. It becomes uniquely different because the new member has added a new dimension to the family unit. This means that the family cannot remain the same, so its first impulse may be to the imminent change. But if the family realizes it will not only be different but also richer in personality and strength, it can welcome the change and capitalize on it.

Another set of changes you can anticipate is rather obvious but not always recognized. Each family member has gotten used to his unique position in the family. He may be the family tease, the merry one, Mr. Fix-it, the singer, the clown. The child who joins the family may compete for one of these roles—perhaps he was a clown in his old family. Naturally this competition will produce tension, but the situation will resolve itself: perhaps one child will end up playing straight man for the other, or perhaps they will learn to share the clown's role. Positions in the family will also change. Like hen-houses, families tend to have a pecking order. How do your children currently relate to each other? And how will the child joining the family affect those relationships? Is he used to a particular position in his old family—only boy, oldest girl, only child? In time the children will establish a new pecking order, but the key is "in time." This is a gradual process, and it takes a sensible adult to know when to try to guide it and when to leave it alone.

Remember, as you anticipate and deal with change, that change is painful and resisted. Recognize, talk about, and take steps to minimize the difficulties that changes bring.

Learning to Talk to Your Child

The quickest, most natural way for most people to get acquainted is to talk to each other. In conversation we exchange important information about ourselves—first in generalities, then in more personal detail. As we share our past and present, our feelings and opinions, we gradually get to know each other.

But children often rely more on the language of deeds than of words. Depending somewhat on age, children tend to reveal much more about themselves by their actions, and they make many decisions about what we are like by carefully assessing our actions. One time a six-year-old named David was spending a few weeks with us while his parents traveled. A friend of David's family was picking him up every morning and taking him to school. One morning, after watching David climb into the car, our son Jeff turned to me and said, "That sure is a nice man." The only thing he knew about the man was what he had observed. The man crossed the street to meet David at our sidewalk, smiled and spoke to him, guided him across the street with his arm loosely around David's shoulders in a friendly fashion, and opened and shut the car door for him before getting into the car himself. These thoughtful actions, which took a little longer and ensured David's safety, impressed our son as those of a "nice man." This incident illustrates the primary importance of actions as you and your new child are getting acquainted.

It is possible, however, to speed up the process of getting acquainted by using conversation, and a reasonably sensitive adult can learn the skills involved in talking to children and adolescents. Of course, you must let the child learn something about *you*, just as you are learning about him; don't let your conversations become one-sided quiz sessions.

How you talk to a child should depend on his age. Techniques that help relax a young child and encourage him to talk will certainly not be right for a teenager. Following are some suggestions to help you gear your approach to the age of the child you want to get to know.

Talking to the pre-school child. If you are attempting to get to know a young child before he comes to live with you, it will probably be helpful if you can talk to the child alone. Talking alone is the best way to discover what the child thinks of himself and his current living situation, and to see how you react to each other. If his mother or another adult is there, or if a talkative brother who tends to answer for him joins you, the child probably will not talk as freely or spontaneously as he would if he were alone with you. The child probably won't want to be alone with you during the first visit, but this should be one eventual goal of your visits if they're meant to help you decide about adding the child to your family. If you've already decided to take the child into your family, the objectives of your visit will be somewhat different—but you'll still need to see the child alone before he moves in.

Young children respond best to adults who are warm and

enthusiastic. They like adults who smile, who use expressive voices—who use a little drama in their conversation. Of course, you don't want to overwhelm the child, but it helps to be lively and to use simple, graphic language. Talk first about the things that have just happened ("Tell me about your ride over here") or about other familiar, safe subjects. (Does he have a pet? What is his favorite game?) If the child is visiting your home, let him explore it, even if he has been there before. You can take his hand and show him something that he noticed during the last visit and comment on it. His first words may be, "Are we going to have bananas again?"—a treat you may have served quite casually a week before and forgotten about. Follow his lead; don't overwhelm him with questions or information.

Of course, you may have to talk quite a bit to keep the conversation going, particularly if the child is unresponsive. If he is, it may be that he doesn't want to talk directly about certain subjects. But with an easy manner and perceptive questions you might get him to talk about these things *indirectly*. If, for example, he won't answer directly when you ask him what things he's afraid of, you might be able to coax out of him an elaborate story about a big dog that once frightened him—his way of trying to find out indirectly if you have a dog.

The conversation will probably go better if you decide ahead of time what things you particularly want to know. You can probably get straight biographical information in other more reliable ways, but talking about sisters, brothers, and the family in general may be a back-door way of learning how he feels about being separated from them and what kind of relationship he has with them. You will probably be interested in learning what he likes or dislikes, what special fears he has, how his "verbal age" compares with his physical age, and a host of other small details which will help you ease his transition from old home to new. Try to get him to talk frankly—about bedtime routines ("I don't like to sleep alone"); about playmates ("Billy is a sissy. He don't like to fight"); about eating habits ("I can get my own cereal"). You can do this best by carefully listening to and guiding the conversation rather than by asking direct questions. Knowing what you are listening for is the key.

If the small child simply will not talk, try doing something with him to get the conversation started. You can get paper and crayons and draw together, using the subject of his drawing to begin a conversation. Or you might try a more physical activity—in fact, a more active child may relax if he plays a vigorous game of tag or works out on a jungle gym, then has a snack with you in a quiet spot.

Talking to the middle-years child. If starting a conversation seems to be the problem with the pre-school child or the adolescent, getting a word in edgewise seems to be the challenge with the middle-years child. Most children from the ages of seven to twelve or thirteen are willing to talk at great length to any adult who will listen. The problem will be to filter the relevant information from the torrent of words you'll hear.

You might think that it would help to take notes as you talk. I would avoid that. Important information will stick with you at least until after the child leaves and you have an opportunity to jot some things down. And remember that the child may suspect that you are taking notes in order to report them to someone else, which could make him unresponsive—at least about anything that's important to him. Even if the child doesn't mind, the distraction of taking notes keeps you from being alert to what is happening at the moment. You may not notice such things as changing facial expressions and restless movements that may be your clues to the child's true feelings about what he's saying.

Once again you need to decide in advance what kind of information you're looking for. You should also realize that a child this old has been wondering about you, too, and would probably like to ask you some fairly specific questions. Fair is fair. Give him a chance to get the information both directly—by letting him freely ask questions—and indirectly—by following his lead if he seems to be trying to steer the conversation in a particular direction.

Keep in mind that school is very important to a child this age. A change in schools—if it's necessary—will be almost as important to him as his change of homes. He might want information about school right away, and appreciate your help in getting it. He will probably ask countless questions: "Is my teacher a man? Do the kids move around to different classes? How many kids are there?" These questions reflect a need not just for information but for your emotional support. Let him know that you believe he will be able to succeed in the new school and that you are going to help him do it. Perhaps during one visit you can plan to make a trip to the school together during his next visit. This will help him feel in greater control of the new situation and reassure him that you do intend to help him in concrete ways.

Do not hesitate to give reassurance in matter-of-fact ways to the child who seems to be covering his doubts about moving with a lot of brave talk. Don't accuse him of fear or directly mention doubts, but do say things like, "I've found most kids hate to leave their old friends, but making new ones is pretty exciting, too. I remember I felt that way when I moved at your age." Use memories from your own childhood to help you identify with this child's experience, and let him know you got help from other people during hard times.

The middle-years child appreciates a warm, expressive conversational style but doesn't like adults to be highly dramatic—even though he sometimes is himself. Usually he will talk more freely if the two of you are alone. But sometimes a girl of ten or twelve will enjoy holding a baby as she talks with you. If the child is reluctant to talk, use an ice-breaker. Have the child help you fix a snack or diaper the baby, or walk to the neighborhood store together for a loaf of bread. Remember that two people don't have to sit in chairs to talk.

Talking to the adolescent. Talking to the adolescent is a difficult art to master—and he probably finds learning to talk to us at least an equal challenge. How difficult it will be to talk with your adolescent will be determined not only by your skill and empathy with his age group. Your communication will also be affected by the reasons he must come to live with you and his attitude toward them, the kinds of experiences he has had, and, most of all, the kinds of relationships he has had with adults.

It will be useless to ask a lot of questions. He will probably notice that he is being carefully quizzed and will also avoid your indirect requests for information. I think a direct approach is best. Come to the point. Say something like, "I want to get to know you, and you probably are curious about me. You want to know what kinds of rules I have, what upsets me, what I will think of your friends, and so on. I'll try to be honest with you, and I'd like you to be honest with me. I'd like you to let me know the things about you that will help us live together." Then follow his lead. Talk about cars or whatever subject comes up, or listen to his gripes about school. Don't be patronizing and fake wisdom about what you don't understand, don't pretend enthusiasm you don't feel. And don't push a subject he wants left alone.

One of the most difficult things to avoid in talking with young people is "coming on like a parent." When we talk to teenagers—no matter what the subject—we seem to have a need to express the parental point of view, and to express it with an air of finality that closes off discussion. I remember one suppertime when our seventeen-year-old was discussing with us a question that had come up in her political science class. Her father and I were taking a viewpoint different from that of her friends, and we thought we were doing so in a perfectly rational and orderly discussion. But all of a sudden she screamed at us, "No matter what we talk about around here, the parents have the last word! I'm not going to bring up class discussions any more!" It was her use of the word *parents* that made us realize we had slipped from a discussion among adults to a discussion between parents and child. Such an incident underscores the fact that adolescents will not share their worries, ideas, or aspirations with adults who always suggest parental approval or censorship in their tone of voice or mannerisms. If your teenager knows your point of view, it is not necessary to state it on every possible occasion.

If an adolescent will soon join or has recently joined your family, you will need to clearly articulate your values and goals, and your perceptions of desirable behavior. When you do this you will want to treat *his* ideas with sensitivity and respect, and allow for compromise. (This subject is further discussed in the section about values in the functional family.)

You should establish an understanding with the adolescent about what is going to happen to the information he shares with you. I think it works best if you primarily reserve the information for you and your spouse, and ask permission to share it with someone else—remembering that the adolescent has a growing need and desire for privacy which should be respected. Naturally you can't give him a blanket promise that you will never repeat anything he says. Avoid setting that trap. But if it seems best to pass on some information to a caseworker, a teacher, or someone else, certainly tell him *why* and try to gain his approval.

It sometimes seems that teenagers talk in a deliberately provocative way, that they are willing to be very "honest" in their appraisal of you and very unwilling to have you respond in kind, that they have forgotten all the rules of logical discourse. If this behavior upsets or perplexes you, remember the difficulty and turmoil of your own teenage years. Try to stay calm and spend more time listening than talking, and you will be surprised how good and meaningful a conversation you can have.

Adding a member to the family is taking a major step. The changes it involves affect every member of the family—in fact, in a fundamental way "family" will not be the same again for any of you or the new child. All of you have mixed feelings about this fact, all of you need opportunities to prepare for the change, all of you will require time to learn to live together. But this new situation also gives your family an opportunity for tremendous growth and increased satisfaction—rewards that make the challenge worthwhile.

CHAPTER 2

ESTABLISHING DEVELOP-MENTAL GOALS FOR YOUR CHILD

Most children grow up in families in which their development proceeds routinely and smoothly. Their parents spend little time consciously considering goals for their development, although in fact they do have a subconscious awareness of what most children accomplish by certain ages. They may also have special goals for their children that are just part of the family's traditional expectations ("Of course he'll graduate from high school"). These parents might find it difficult to write out in words an answer to this question: "What goals would you like your boy or girl to reach by the time he enters first grade?" Nonetheless, their families are probably functioning with goals that specific in mind—just as your family is.

If you are bringing a new child into your family, it may be helpful if you are even more specific about your expectations and more aware of your evaluations of the child's developmental progress. This is true for several reasons.

First of all, it is quite possible that the child has joined your family after an upsetting experience or a series of unsettling events. His move from the home into which he was born to your home is still another serious upheaval in his life. For these reasons it's worth considering in a systematic way how these experiences have affected his development, and what you may need to do to overcome specific lags or trouble spots.

Quite a number of children join a new family after several years of inadequate care or willful abuse, or a series of moves from one living arrangement to another. They may have suffered the loss of a series of parent figures as baby-sitters came and went or as they were shifted around from one relative's home to another. Such years of childhood stress affect these children in many different ways. One may be healthy and friendly but noticeably lagging behind his peers in intellectual development. Another may be smaller and less coordinated than other children his age. If such a child comes to live with you, you cannot assume that he will automatically "catch up" simply because his home environment is improved. He will probably need extra help and attention.

Occasionally all seems well at the time a child joins the family, but difficulties crop up as the child leaves home for first grade, or becomes an adolescent. If this happens, it is worth examining your child's history to discover whether his trouble is simply the ordinary stress a child may experience and master during these transitional periods, or if it is related to earlier problems buried unsolved.

Another reason for carefully investigating your child's history is that a disturbingly large number of children do not receive good medical attention. This tends to be especially true of children raised in poor or single-parent families, and children who have had to adapt to a succession of parent figures. Systematically evaluating your child's physical development can reveal possible medical needs.

What you may not know about child-rearing also makes it vital for you to carefully consider the present development of the child you will parent, and the goals you set for him. When my husband and I began caring for children other than our biological own, we were a young married couple with no experience beyond caring for our infant daughter. We lacked the fund of knowledge built up by raising children over a period of years—knowledge that would have told us what to expect in behavior and development, what were danger signals and what were false alarms. Because of our inexperience, we often became concerned about the wrong things.

Even if you have raised other children, you may have forgotten much of what you learned about child development, or you may find this child much different from your other children in personality and manner. You will need to evaluate goals and development with his particular needs in mind, not only guided by your past experience.

Of course you can't raise a child "by the book," but neither can you raise him without adequate knowledge. The following pages provide an overview of that knowledge; they couldn't possibly spell out normal child development in detail or outline comprehensive goals for child-rearing. I will make general statements about the three basic age groups—pre-school, middle-years, and adolescent—and point out potential problem areas for the child growing up with a new family. If you are an inexperienced parent, or will be parenting a child of an age you're not familiar with (if you are adding a teenager to your very young family, for instance), I hope you will do additional reading. It will also help you to talk to seasoned parents and teachers who are working with children of about the same age as your child. (Don't let these conversations become gossip and gripe sessions; keep the discussions constructive.)

The discussion following will include brief descriptions of typical physical, intellectual, and emotional/social development for each principal age group. Naturally these kinds of development—though separated to make the discussion easier—are interconnected. They also occur unevenly: a child may forge ahead in one kind of development and lag behind in another. Of course, unifying and affecting all of the child's growth is his religious or spiritual development, which is most important of all.

Developmental Goals for the Pre-school child

Physical development. Proper physical development is directly related to good physical health. Though you may have a fairly good idea of what a healthy child is, and the conviction that your child is healthy, every pre-school child—however apparently healthy—should be seen regularly by a physician. The doctor can not only treat illnesses but also check to be certain that the child's physical development is normal. He will notice if the child is developing a peculiar walk to compensate for a muscle deformity which could be corrected, or if repeated ear infections are leading to hearing loss. His questioning of you plus his regular professional observation of the child can help him determine that all is going well—or that additional medical attention is needed.

Health officials are dismayed that many children are reaching school age without being immunized against polio, measles, and other serious childhood diseases for which immunization is readily available. The child joining your family may need immunization. Check his records; if they show no reason why he shouldn't be immunized, be sure to arrange for this important protection.

Other preventive measures are important, too. If the child has a serious loss of vision or hearing, his doctor will probably notice and suggest further tests. But remember that less extensive loss is not always obvious in a routine office examination. For that reason a child should have his hearing and vision tested by the time he enters school. His teeth should be checked regularly by a dentist from the time he is two or three, the age range during which he has gained all of his temporary teeth.

Medical check-ups, immunization, dental care, and special testing—all these are expensive. If your family budget cannot cover them, you may be able to get outside help if you are persistent. Local communities vary widely in the amount of low-cost care they provide. Ask your local medical or dental society for information about where to go for help. Call the Family Service Agency or your local welfare office. You may have to swallow your pride to make these calls, but for the sake of the child's good health, do it. And look for other possible options, too. Sometimes local colleges or universities have student-staffed clinics open to the public. A community school for the handicapped may give tests that determine what children need their help. But perhaps the best place to start is with your family physician (if you have one). Remember that untreated problems have a way of getting worse—sometimes becoming uncorrectable—and usually require eventual attention that is much more expensive than prompt attention. In the meantime the child may be enduring an unnecessary handicap.

Besides ensuring that the pre-school child gets good medical attention, you can take several other steps to ensure his good physical health.

Because of his rapid growth the young child needs a balanced daily diet. But the child entering your home will have definite food preferences which may indicate indulgent eating habits. If he is used to irregular meals and frequent snacks of soft drinks, salty foods, and candy bars, you will need to improve his diet gradually. Do not immediately take away everything he likes and begin to insist he eat exactly what you think he should have. This may create an eating problem and interfere with the child's adjustment to you and your home.

Use the plan you put into general practice to permanently improve your child's eating habits. Include plenty of proteins, grains, fruits, vegetables, and milk. Wean him away from refined sugars and starches and from excessive amounts of fat. If he needs snacks for between-meal energy, try to encourage him to eat foods that have vitamins and minerals as well as quick-energy calories—an apple instead of a candy bar, an icy glass of orange juice instead of a can of pop. Including a wide variety of foods in his diet is a good way to ensure that he gets all the nutritional elements his body needs. If your child develops a finicky appetite—which some children do from time to time—he may sabotage your plans. But if other family members continue to eat a variety of foods with obvious enjoyment, the child will probably begin imitating them.

You should also pay close attention to your child's muscle development. Good muscle development usually occurs as the child alternates running and playing with periods of quiet activity. Muscular growth is cyclical: as a child uses his muscles they become stronger and more usable, which tends to encourage the child to use them still more. For maximum development a child needs to alternate "large muscle activities" with "small muscle activities." Large muscle activity ensures a sturdy body, good posture, and general physical coordination. Small muscle activity develops good eye-hand coordination and the ability to manipulate small objects, such as scissors, crayons, pencils, and eating utensils.

A child needs space for large muscle activities: running, jumping, climbing. A child also needs objects that encourage him to play hard—a tricycle or scooter to ride, large balls for playing catch, a pool of some kind if possible. Always important, of course, are playmates, whom your child can interact with physically—in a vigorous game of tag or hide-and-seek—*and* socially. You may discover that your child doesn't enjoy vigorous play; my husband and I have worked with a few children who didn't. One boy had grown fearful of the roughness of older children; another child was so near-sighted that she wasn't physically confident until she was fitted with glasses. Right now we have a child who apparently hasn't done much hard playing and needs to be tempted into learning how to enjoy it. If your child shies away from vigorous activity, try to encourage him to play harder—but do so gently and gradually.

You can devise all kinds of small muscle activities for your child. Let him work with a homemade ball of salt dough (a local nursery school will be glad to share the recipe over the phone). Let him paint with a brush and plain water on colored paper, or whack away at old magazines with blunt scissors. (Make sure the scissors will actually cut. Some sold are so poorly made that even an adult would have trouble using them.) And remember that even very young children can be taught to clean up the mess they make—another good small muscle activity. This may exasperate you at first, but your initial patience will be rewarded: your child will develop valuable skills while he's learning about responsibility, and while he's amusing himself you can read a book or call a friend. When a rainy day keeps your child inside, give him a "pounding board" and a few nails. This gives a child a good outlet for his excess energy and good exercise for both his large and small muscles.

Physical development and the development of muscle control tend to follow a pattern: they move from the head downward and from the center of the body outward. That is, the child can hold his head erect before he can sit, and can make large, awkward movements with his arms before he can make small movements with his fingers. (There is wisdom in the folk saying, "You have to crawl before you can walk.") As you assess your child's muscle development, remember that, although the *pattern* of growth tends to be the same for all children, the *rate* of growth may vary. But if you think your child is definitely lagging behind in some way, ask your doctor to examine him.

Helping the pre-school child develop habits to maintain health and cleanliness is also important. Generally speaking, a child who is ready to enter school has bowel and bladder control (although bed-wetting at night is still very common) and is able to make trips to the bathroom unassisted. He should know how to brush his teeth, something he should be doing regularly. Teach him to wash his hands before eating and after trips to the bathroom; give him his own towel and washcloth to use and rehang himself. You should also encourage him to dress and feed himself, and to take care of himself in other basic ways. Because his physical skills are less than perfect, the results may be less than perfect. But no matter how uncoordinated he seems, give him plenty of chances to perform these practical tasks, because they stimulate both his physical and mental growth. Be sure to develop the habit of noticing and commenting favorably on his efforts to be self-sufficient. Never use the words "clumsy" or "awkward," whether you are talking to him or describing him to yourself or others.

The following summary provides a rough sketch of the physically average five-year-old. (Keep in mind that some variation is perfectly normal.) Motor skills are quite well-developed: the child can run, hop, skip, pedal a trike, and throw a ball a good distance. He has the skill and confidence to climb a ladder or a jungle gym, to walk a low ledge. He likes swings, scooters, and anything else he can pedal, push, or pull. He can dress himself—managing buttons and ties—feed himself, and set a table. He can sing a simple song, follow an easy rhythm, and join in games and activities with other children. He is vigorous and active, but he also tires in a relatively short time and needs frequent periods of quiet play. He eats three meals a day and between-meal snacks; he needs about eleven hours of sleep each night. His measurable growth is impressive: his height has doubled, and he is five times heavier than he was at birth.

Intellectual development. Although we can basically agree about how to set goals for a child's physical development, and how to evaluate his physical progress, it is much more difficult to make pronouncements about "normal" intellectual development—for any age. This is especially true for the pre-school child. His intellectual development is extremely hard to measure; in fact, it is difficult to determine what encourages this development in the first place. But the famous Swiss psychologist Jean Piaget has helped unravel the mystery.

Piaget has proposed that a child's intellectual development occurs in stages distinguished by particular kinds of behavior. He labels the first stage sensori-motor, a stage that lasts until about age two. During this period the baby or toddler is investigating objects to get information about them. He puts his toys in his mouth, shakes them to hear them rattle. He pushes, pulls, squeezes, tastes, and smells. In fact, the intelligent child at this age is using *all* of his senses—smell, touch, taste, sight, and hearing—to learn about the world.

We can encourage a baby to use his senses by trying to be certain that the world he reaches out to responds in some way. There must be voices to hear, objects to manipulate, actions to watch. My husband and I were vividly reminded of this fact when a six-month-old child came to live with us. She lay so still and quiet that we thought she was deaf. But in a few weeks she was an active, cooing, gurgling baby. She was not deaf at all, but apparently her early environment had been so barren of response that she had simply given up trying to use her senses.

By age three or four the young child is in what Piaget calls the early pre-operational stage. Now he is able to associate words with things. He has played peek-a-boo in a hundred ways and situations, and he now knows that objects have permanence—they don't disappear just because he cannot see them. He also recognizes shapes, sizes, and textures, and he begins to remember these characteristics. He does not have to handle objects each time he sees them to know they have these features. At the same time he does not yet have the capacity to mentally analyze and compare the characteristics of objects. He cannot think of the blue block as *light* blue in comparison to a darker block unless he sees them side by side. He also thinks egocentrically. That is, he sees objects from his viewpoint and cannot imagine what they look like from your viewpoint. He also thinks his way is the only way to see things. It's no wonder, then, a child at two or three seems obstinate, determined to have things "his way." His self-absorbed stubbornness simply indicates the stage of his intellectual development.

Though he remains in the pre-operational stage until he is seven or eight, the older pre-school child does begin to think intuitively and to be aware of other points of view. He can also follow steps in a process by remembering them, although he does not always understand the order of the process. His thoughts and actions are not always well-coordinated: he may forget to turn the hose away from himself before he turns the faucet on and get an unexpected shower, even though he knows that water will come out when he turns the faucet handle. If asked about his actions, he may not be able to answer the question, "Why did you do that?" He is unable to reconstruct his mental steps. During this stage a child will learn best by directly participating in activities, and less well by getting only verbal instructions.

We usually assess the older child's intelligence by evaluating his language skills. Even if we measure his skill in manipulating objects (putting pegs into holes, stacking blocks, matching colors), we are still measuring his language skills, because how well he performs the activities is directly related to how well he processes the directions in his mind. By following the growth of these language skills, we can trace a child's intellectual development.

The number and variety of sounds an infant makes is the most important single predictor of his adult intelligence. The attention the child gets when he makes sounds encourages him to use language, which he learns by imitation. Actually the very young baby makes all of the sounds needed to speak *any* language in the world; he simply drops the ones he doesn't hear in the language around him. At this early age his language growth can be retarded by two kinds of people—by adults who are overly fussy and respond to him too soon and too frequently, and by adults who do not respond to him at all. If adults constantly fuss over a child, he never gets a chance to find out that it is *what* he does that brings about a certain response. If adults refuse to respond to him, he begins to think that language is not a tool, and may stop using it. He needs adults who realize from the beginning that communication involves both talking and listening. Singing to the infant is also helpful, since it lets him hear tones, pitches, and high and low volume.

By age two a child can usually form simple two-word sentences made up of a noun and a verb and can vary his inflection to let you know what he means—e.g., "Cat gone" or "Cat gone?" He has a vocabulary of 250 to 300 words and understands many more than he uses. The language he knows is very important to him, because he uses it as a tool to analyze his experiences and attach meaning to them. You can increase his ability to use and understand language by giving him simple, clear directions to follow, by speaking in short sentences, and by naming objects to him as you use them. Remember that the culture he is part of will begin to affect how he acquires language, too. He senses what is off-color (and may test his perception by watching your reaction when he repeats a "naughty" word or story). Guided by the characteristics peculiar to the language he is learning, he recognizes slang, uses word order to affect meaning, and begins to use synonyms. If he has learned one language but must learn a second language when he goes to school or enters your home, he may appear less intelligent than he actually is. Remember that his skill with his *native* language is the real indicator of his intelligence.

From the time he is two until the time he is five, the child's vocabulary increases rapidly. In fact, many five-year-olds can use 2,500 words. If you encourage a child to use these words as he tries to express his ideas or feelings, you will be encouraging both his expressive skills and his intellectual development. Try to encourage pretending, too. The imagination a child uses to "make believe" will be the eventual source of creative painting, writing, and other kinds of vivid self-expression. But even more important than what you do is your general attitude toward what your child does. If you believe in his ability, he gains confidence in himself and the courage to try increasingly complex and challenging things.

Occasionally you will need to correct a child's word usage

or grammar, but most of the time he will learn best if you give him good speech patterns to follow and keep corrections to a minimum. You should also resist the impulse to constantly "help" the child who stutters; the best thing to do is to ignore this slight impediment. Stuttering peaks at about age four, and usually goes away all by itself. My husband and I have a son who stuttered when he was younger. A friend of ours in speech therapy asked us to drop the word *stutter* from our vocabulary, and insist that others also ignore it. He also asked us to listen patiently to our child. We took his advice, and it worked. One day, in fact, my little boy came to me and haltingly explained that the little boy across the street stuttered—he had no idea that he had the same speech characteristic! By the time he was six, the child was talking constantly without hesitating at all.

In recent years an interesting question has been much debated: which influences a person more—genetic inheritance or environment? The question probably never will be settled. In any case it is worth remembering that intellectual development is a combination of different factors. We do inherit certain abilities. But we also enter an environment with primary influence: it gives or withholds certain experiences and provides or denies in certain ways. The opportunities we have to use our skills vary, as does the responsiveness of people around us. We thus respond to parts of our environment and ignore other parts. Especially in problem-solving, adapting, memorizing, reasoning, and making judgments—all factors in what we call intelligence—experience is more important than genetics. In short, the capabilities we are born with are strategically affected by the environment in which we live.

The intellectual goals for the pre-schooler can be simply summarized. He should be able to listen to a story or look through a picture book; capable of performing a simple task by following directions; familiar with the names and characteristics of objects he uses or sees frequently; and able to express his ideas and feelings to sympathetic adults.

Emotional/social development. A child's emotional and social development are interdependent, and usually parallel each other. This is true from birth. The first developments in a child's emotional life take place as he and the mother figure interact. The atmosphere and manner in which the infant receives physical care are as important as the care itself. In fact, routine physical care is not enough to ensure his proper development: he needs to receive that care in a generally pleasant atmosphere from a person who is warm, loving, and attentive. This is the beginning of both emotional and social development for the child.

Almost immediately a mother recognizes the distinct personality of her baby—he is active or passive, fussy or calm. The mother and the other family members need to respect this personality—to appreciate the baby for himself—if they are to establish a good emotional relationship with him.

But during his second year the child must begin to learn to put his distinctiveness in perspective—he must begin to learn how to live socially. He must first of all be weaned. Weaning is his introduction to social demands: someone else—not him—now determines the conditions of his feeding. Even if he has been on a feeding schedule, this is a big change. Gradual, tender weaning helps him to accept it.

Later in the second year the family increasingly cannot or will not meet all of the baby's demands. Yet his growing sense of self tends to make it harder for him to give in now than it was earlier or will be later. Late in the second year the family will probably initiate toilet training. The child's response will depend on his previous social/emotional experience. If his needs have been met in a warm, accepting way, he will probably be ready to meet this demand. Patience, gentleness, and a willingness to accept some relapses will pay off in easier, faster toilet training, with less wear and tear on the whole family. Remember that the young child seems to have an inborn desire to master new situations; capitalize on this rather than stirring up his balkiness by being insistent and authoritative.

By now most children have learned a few ways to manipulate their parents to get what they want. If tricks like temper tantrums and "breath holding" get results, a child may use them often. If these emotional upheavals continue with frequency, parents should examine the demands placed on the child to make sure they're reasonable. Perhaps he needs less tiring play schedules, fewer persons to listen to, or less rigid discipline. But if parents are convinced that their expectations are fair, they should maintain them even during these storms of temper.

At the age of three and after the young child has three skills that allow him to be more social: he can walk, he can talk, and he is toilet-trained. For the next few years his social world will change and grow rapidly, and he will learn how to share. First he learns to "share" people. When he was younger, his parents catered to his demands. But now he becomes aware that he can't remain the center of attention—a new baby demands some of his parents' time, perhaps, and prompts this realization. Similarly, he learns to share his mother with his father. If he is in a day care center or a play school, he learns to share his teacher with other children. He also is capable of understanding how to share toys and take turns.

Nonetheless, there is often a great deal of fighting and rivalry between children three, four, and five years old. This frequently grows out of situations in which a child feels unequally loved, or in which limitations set are haphazard or rules are not fairly applied to all children. The unfavored child becomes hostile and aggressive; the favored child is quick to exploit his advantage, and may do much tattling and teasing. The adults in charge must realize how they might be contributing—inadvertently or otherwise—to the problem. And they should recognize that particularly difficult situations can develop when a new child joins an established family. (The problem of fighting and rivalry is more thoroughly discussed in Chapter 5.)

Many children in this age range have imaginary companions, especially if they play alone much of the time. If your child has such "friends," don't worry about it: he is simply entertaining himself with his imagination. Just try to make sure that he plays with other children part of the time.

A child this age also begins to learn society's ground rules. He learns the names of his emotions. He learns that he is supposed to be shamed by certain things. He begins to understand what is expected of him and to realize that he does not always want to do what is expected. He learns to approve and disapprove. During this time the child needs to have sensitive adults help him acknowledge and accept these feelings, and teach him socially acceptable ways to handle them. Because he is very vulnerable and does not know how to protect himself or fight back well, he can be hurt by adults who are verbally cruel to him, or who take out their frustrations on him. Adults who resort to sarcasm, belittlement, shaming, and name-calling can do embittering, long-lasting damage to a child. For *positive* emotional growth the child needs adults around him who recognize their feelings, discuss them with the child, and show him how to cope with them acceptably.

In brief, goals for the social/emotional development of the pre-school child are several: He should be able to distinguish among and respond in the close relationships he has with special people, usually his family; be able to play happily with other children with only occasional adult intervention or help; be able to play alone, using his imagination and available toys and books to enjoy himself; be able to trust adults and seek help from them; and be able to manage emotions like anger and fear reasonably well with help.

Developmental Goals for the Middle-years Child

Numerous researchers have spent lifetimes investigating the development of pre-school children, and reams of material have been written about the adolescent. In comparison, there are few researchers and little material exploring the development of the child from age six through age ten or eleven. The child is in elementary school during this time—called "the middle years" and most easily distinguished from the earlier or later years by the quiet pace at which they move. But though it is quieter, much is happening in the child's life during this period. In some ways it is like middle age: the child, like the adult, is industriously using and managing the skills he has acquired to "get the job done." The strategic question is this: How well will he emerge from these middle years to face the stress of adolescence?

Physical development. The child in elementary school is

in a period of comparatively slow growth. He looks slimmer as the amount and distribution of his baby fat change, and his muscles become stronger and better connected to his bones. His skeleton and his muscular structure are not yet mature, however, and are still easy to injure. In addition, his heart is smaller in relation to his body than at any other time in his life. For these reasons a child this age should avoid very strenuous competitive sports and concentrate on general physical development.

The grade-school child is healthier than he was as a pre-schooler. The seemingly endless colds are fewer. He has fewer ear infections, too. The reason? As the lower face grows a child's ear tubes slant downward at a greater angle and germs enter less easily. His digestive system is also less easily upset.

But, even though he is healthier than he was (or will be later), the middle-years child will still spend an average of eight days a year sick in bed. You may wonder why—particularly if your family is healthy. The reason: though they are not sick as often as pre-schoolers, middle-years children contract the widest variety of serious illnesses of any age group. Affecting these statistics is the fact that the quality of children's health is directly related to the quality of medical care they receive—and many children in our country do not receive good, systematic professional care. Their frequent and longer illnesses are reflected in the sick-day average. (In fact, children average three bouts with acute illnesses per year, but only about half of these illnesses are actually treated by a doctor.) Another principal factor in the sick-day average is respiratory infection: it accounts for three out of five lost school days.

What can you do to minimize this problem? You can exercise preventive health care, and take your child to see a doctor if he becomes seriously ill. You can also minimize the *length* of an illness with good convalescent care: if the body gets good nutrition and extra rest, it can restore itself more quickly to its normal condition.

The middle-years child doesn't need to eat as often as the younger child does. Because his growth is slower, he needs fewer calories. During these years adults need to help him distinguish between high-calorie foods without substantial food value and those which will give him both energy and important supplies of protein, vitamins, and minerals. If the child's eating habits are poor, he may become overweight. In fact, obesity is a serious problem in the elementary school group. But if a child this age develops good eating habits, they will probably stay with him—even if he goes through a temporary lapse in high school.

Regular eye examinations are a necessity for the middle-years child because his chances of developing vision defects increase every year during this period. Regular tests ensure the prompt discovery and correction of any defect. Regular dental check-ups are also important. One in four children in this age range has not been to a dentist, but the charts on your dentist's wall will show that the average middle-years child has numerous cavities which should have attention.

A child enters elementary school with a good range of physical skills. He can jump, run, climb, hop, skip, and throw a ball and catch it (sometimes!) when it is thrown back. During these years he will develop all of the basic skills needed to play the games popular in his age group. He will be willing to practice incessantly to learn these skills, especially if he is encouraged by friends and adults. Some of these activities will require large muscle skills, some finer coordination, some a combination of both. But play does more than develop physical skills: good physical education programs actually contribute to children's academic success, especially in the later elementary years when they prefer large muscle activities.

You may be discouraged as your child this age jumps from one activity to another, seldom, it seems, finishing anything or mastering thoroughly what he started. This tendency peaks when the child is about nine—the nine-year-old is interested in a wider variety of activities than any other age child. In fact, if you provide a list of every activity you can think of to a roomful of nine-year-olds, it is likely that each activity will be chosen as a favorite by at least one of the children. Later your child will selectively limit his activities and will try to excel in fewer games. But right now he wants to try them all.

Physical goals for the middle-years child reveal his increasing maturity. He should be able to take increasing responsibility for his own good health—developing nutritious eating habits, bathing and brushing his teeth regularly, getting adequate sleep and exercise. He should be able to try out a wide range of activities and learn the skills involved in the games and sports of childhood. He should also be able to develop a body which satisfies his need to be and feel physically competent and attractive.

Intellectual development. The intellectual development of the middle-years child, like that of the pre-school child, does not occur in a vacuum: it is directly related to his physical development. As he has experiences and gains information through his physical senses, he accumulates a store of memories that he can tap to understand new situations. By using words to store and retrieve this information, he can use what he has learned more easily and precisely. A picture becomes a picture of a cream-colored house with slate blue trim; a smell becomes the sweet fragrance of a rose. The biggest task of the middle-years child is to learn to think better—to organize what he knows and add to it, to learn to make comparisons and put things together in new ways. To do this, he needs language and the ability to use it as a tool when he thinks.

When he is about seven, the child begins to develop new mental capabilities. One of these is *flexibility*. He can now mentally move back and forth in time. He can compare the past with the present. His thinking also becomes less self-oriented and inflexible: he can look at situations from other points of view. For instance: the pre-school child who was once bitten by a dog may continue to think that all dogs bite, that they intend to bite him in particular, and that the only thing the dog is interested in is biting him. But an older child is able to distinguish between a dog which bit him in the past and the one he now sees, to realize that the dog is not about to bite him just because he imagines the dog might, and to remember that dogs also like to chase squirrels—and this one may be completely engaged in doing just that. This new ability to think flexibly greatly increases the child's feeling of control in the situation.

Another new cognitive skill that the middle-years child will develop is the ability to *reverse*. He can now imagine an action and then decide not to do it. He can start performing a task mentally, stop in the middle of it, and try doing it another way—all without actually doing anything physically. The great advantage here is that thoughts are reversible, whereas actions are not. This ability to think through an action before performing it is another mental skill that gives the child greater control of situations. Think of the power a child feels when he can mentally disassemble a toy and then realize that he can't put it together again—all without doing any damage.

When he is about seven the child enters what Piaget calls the concrete operations stage. The child is still acting upon objects, but now he can do more than manipulate them physically—he can translate them into ideas and mental symbols. Classifying and ordering are the principal mental operations the child performs in this stage.

Classifying is the skill involved in grouping things according to their common characteristics. A very young child calls almost anything on the end of a stem "flower." But the middle-years child learns how to be much more specific. He distinguishes flowers from weeds, he separates flowers with smell from flowers without smell, he groups flowers by their colors. He can look at the red flowers in a bouquet and decide whether or not they are the dominant color in the bunch.

When a pre-schooler learns a new physical skill, he uses it over and over. I can remember when our third child mastered the twelve-foot slide. Again and again she climbed the ladder to race down that slide. The next day she could barely lift her sore legs to climb stairs. In the same way the middle-years child gets carried away with his new ability to classify—and that is one of the reasons he loves to collect. At first his collections are very general. He may pick up all pretty stones until his room overflows with them. But soon he will probably become more selective and collect only one type of stone—fossils, for example. Later he may search through books to learn how to classify his fossils by age or type. Some middle-years children have half a dozen collections of objects like these. It is their way of practicing and mastering their newly acquired skill.

Ordering is the second operation the grade-school child learns. This involves using some sort of standard to put things into proper relation to each other. By the standard of time, the child puts events in order; in this way he develops his sense of history, both personal and general. He also orders by length, by height, by space occupied, or by weight. Many of his comments about classmates concern who is tallest, who can throw a ball "fartherest," who has the most marbles, who eats the most, etc.

All these ways of ordering appear in rather crude form at first—some of them, in fact, are not completely mastered by the middle-years child. For instance, he cannot estimate the passage of time very accurately and does not significantly improve in this skill until he is older. He really does not have a very clear idea of the time involved when you say, "Be home in half an hour." He needs to gauge a time period by the clock. Similarly, a child this age has little understanding of longer periods of time—ages, eras, etc.—until he is about eight, and even then his comprehension of them is poor. He may think "the olden days" refer to your childhood, not pioneer days, as many a parent has been surprised to learn. In fact, he is not actually ready to study history in a formal sense until he is about sixteen, though of course he can learn about various cultures and historical events before that age.

Besides learning how to order and classify, the middle-years child grasps the concept of *conservation*. The pre-school child is able to realize that objects have permanence—that is, that they are not gone just because he can't see them anymore. The elementary school child is engaged in learning that objects can change their size and shape and still be quantitatively the same. If you pour two glasses of juice for a small child and his friend, he will not believe they hold the same amount if one glass is tall and skinny and the other is short and fat. And he will not believe it even if you pour the juice into a measuring cup to prove it to him. But the middle-years child can grasp this concept. He knows that a graham cracker which is broken into two pieces is quantitatively the same as the original cracker, or that a stick of melted butter is a half-cup if the original stick was a half-cup. The child learns this concept most easily if he has many experiences illustrating it. Once again practice is important. Just keep in mind that premature practice—encouraged before the child is old enough to grasp the concept—won't be very productive.

The school subject which depends very heavily on classifying, ordering, and conservation is mathematics. If a child dislikes or doesn't understand math in school, it may be because he has had few experiences that let him practically apply these concepts. That's why letting your new daughter experiment with recipes may help her more with her math than hours of drill.

The middle-years child also develops what can be called his own *cognitive style.* If you have parented a number of children, it is quite likely that you are aware that each child has his own way of analyzing situations and attacking problems. Psychologist Jerome Kagan characterizes children as "splitters" or "lumpers" according to their basic style of perception. A splitter is analytical; he tends to take things apart, to pay attention to details. A lumper groups details together, looking at the total picture rather than its individual components.

Styles of perception can also be described as "impulsive" and "reflective." The impulsive child would answer problems on a math test quickly, almost "sensing" the answers, and would make more errors. On the other hand, the reflective child would take the problems apart in his mind, try out different answers to them, and give answers that would be more likely to be right—though he may be too slow to get all of the problems done. Neither way of thinking characterizes one sex or the other, though there are more boys who are extremely impulsive, and more girls who are extremely reflective. In addition, cognitive style and physical style seem to be related—i.e., a child who acts impulsively tends to think impuslively.

As a parent you should realize a few things about cognitive style. You should realize that you can probably influence your child's cognitive style somewhat by your style of parenting. If this possibility interests you, you can investigate it further by reading psychology books. It helps to realize that each style has its advantages—neither is necessarily preferable to the other. Analytic style is related to success in fields like mathematics and physics; non-analytic style is associated with success in the arts or social sciences.

You should also realize that understanding your child's style can help you appreciate him more and avoid unnecessary conflict. If you tend to be impulsive, a reflective child may bother you. You might be tempted to call him lazy or slow. On the other hand, if you are reflective an impulsive child might annoy you. You might be tempted to constantly nag him to slow down. But if you recognize and respect the differences between you as fundamental differences in perception and personality, you will be much less likely to have such problems, and much more able to appreciate your child's distinctive personality.

Another factor influencing a child's style is the sense he primarily uses to get information about the world. One depends more heavily on what he sees, another learns best through what he hears, another may be quite dependent on touching and handling. The child needs to be provided with all kinds of sensory experiences so that he can decide which of his senses is the best teacher. As he grows older he gets better at using all of his senses and effectively combining the information he gets from them.

Although a child this age is becoming increasingly sophisticated mentally, you cannot really expect mature responses from him. He has a particular cognitive limitation that you should be aware of. Earlier I mentioned that the preschool child has a limited point of view: he does not have the ability to see things as you see them. In somewhat the same way, the middle-years child draws conclusions that he sometimes clings to illogically. He forms a hypothesis that seems to explain a situation to him. Once it is formed, he tends to hang on to it for dear life, ignoring any evidence that contradicts it and looking for any evidence that supports it.

An example will clarify this cognitive limitation. Not very long after she moves in with you, you refuse to let your new middle-years child have something she wants. Jeannie then develops the explanation "She doesn't want me here" to account for your failure to give her the item. She may then ignore all of the other kindnesses you have shown her (evidence contrary to her hypothesis), and look for anything in your treatment of her that might support her idea that you don't want her. For this reason she perceives even your most ordinary actions as signs of rejection. You may be quite baffled by the change in her behavior that her attitude will certainly cause. Fortunately, if you can figure out her hypothesis and work directly with that and the incident on which she based it ("You seem to feel that I don't want you here because I wouldn't buy you skates"), you may be able to convince her that she jumped to the wrong conclusion.

It is worth emphasizing the point that children are not miniature adults in their thinking processes. If an adult always keeps in mind what thought processes the middle-years child is able to use, he will be less likely to label a child as careless, stubborn, lazy, or unreasonable. These labels are useless in changing behavior, and may be very unfair besides.

The child's intellectual development, of course, continues to be closely related to his language development. His growing language skills help to develop his thinking processes, and, in turn, his ability to think better improves his use and grasp of the language. The very young child's egocentric thinking is reflected in his egocentric language. He uses words in a self-absorbed expression of his wants and ideas. But the elementary school child becomes increasingly interested in using language to *exchange* meaning. His speech is social: he struggles hard to understand what you mean by a word and to use the right word to let you know what he means. He still uses egocentric speech (speech for himself alone), but now he uses it silently. He gives himself directions, thinks through problems, regulates himself, and gives himself praise or blame. This silent speech is enormously important to the child, especially important to the development of his self-image. If you have a child this age, you can ensure that he has a good "silent speech" vocabulary by at first encouraging him to talk to himself out loud. Particularly encourage him to talk positively, to give himself encouragement and praise. (Chapter 5 discusses encouragement in greater detail.)

The child's aptitude for social speech grows in proportion to the opportunities he has to talk with good listeners who help him clarify his ideas and who listen respectfully to his theories. It is particularly important that his family encourage conversation. If your child's conversations "wander," remember that a child this age is still developing his ability to stay with a topic. And remember that even some adults have trouble sticking to the subject!

The middle-years child improves his language skills in other ways, too: he usually improves his articulation. About seventy-five percent of all children who enter kindergarten pronounce at least one sound in the language incorrectly. But by age seven most children can pronounce all of the sounds correctly. However, it is important to note that the child who makes errors in articulation in first, second, and third grade usually still makes them in fourth grade. This child usually makes other mistakes with words, too. Unfortunately, there is no guarantee that this problem will correct itself as the child grows older. Because clear and correct pronunciation of sounds is essential for proper language development, a parent should listen to his child's speech carefully. If a child is not pro-nouncing sounds correctly by age seven, he should get speech therapy as soon as possible.

The middle-years child uses language to help create a private world he shares only with other children. With them he shares jokes, rhymes, and riddles. Chants for games and rhymes for jumping rope are learned from other children, used a few years, passed on, and almost forgotten. But they survive nonetheless. Has it surprised you to pass a school yard and hear your daughter and her friends using a jump-rope song you remember using, but never taught her? Many of these special chants of childhood are in fact hundreds of years old, and are used in widely separated countries.

Some of these chants have power over the middle-years child because he believes—or half-believes—in word magic. He suspects that words may be able to change reality. This ex-plains children's use of name-calling, and the fury with which the slandered child responds. It also explains their use of chants to ward off bad things. Although these chants aren't very logical, few children can be talked out of their belief in them. Most children simply use these chants for a while and outgrow them, so no harm is done. But a few children become obsessed with such chants, and begin to fear their possible consequence—e.g., a child anxiously avoids the cracks in the sidewalk because he wonders if it really *would* break his mother's back if he stepped on one. In fact, once in a while a child will think that word magic has something to do with his losing a parent or being moved to a new home. If this is true of the child joining your family, he may need some counseling.

A middle-years child also uses language in a special way to tell jokes. As the mother of a four-year-old knows, a small child's idea of a joke is a long, rambling story which from an adult's point of view has no particular point. To the middle-years child, such stories aren't funny anymore. His humorous story is concise and has a punch line; he seems especially fond of "moron jokes." These probably relieve some of the tension for the middle-years child, who is working hard to master so many skills. He is concerned with doing well, with being smart—and he is afraid of failing. These jokes lessen the pressure he feels, because in them he definitely is not the moron—quite likely an older child or an adult plays that role. In fact, the middle-years child often disparages adults in his jokes. This seems to be his way of reassuring himself and his friends that it is okay not to know everything. His jokes tend to be too crude for older children or adults, but they are similar to adult jokes in some ways and almost always have a surprise ending. This appeals to the child because he prides himself on knowing something you don't know.

A child's changing use of his imagination is another factor in his intellectual development. Because he is so busy with the real world, the middle-years child tends to use his imagination less than the pre-school child does. He is preoccupied with controlled thinking. But he still expresses his imagination, especially in his language and his humor. This free-flowing imagination allows him to be creative in the true sense—he produces not great quantities of copied ideas less perfect than the original, but truly unique and original work.

The intellectual goals for the middle-years child are numerous. He should develop the cognitive skills of classifying and ordering, and have many opportunities to practice them. He should also develop flexibility in his thinking processes so that he can mentally perform actions. In addition, he should develop his own cognitive style without becoming either extremely impulsive or reflexive—a style that should be understood and respected by parents and other adults. To help, parents should provide a child with a variety of sensory experiences that help him use all of his senses while he's learning. They should also be aware of and respect his new cognitive skills—and his cognitive limitations. And they should ensure that he has opportunities to use and improve his mastery of language, to develop his sense of humor with sensitive adults, to join the special language world of children, and to express his unique personality in imaginative ways.

Emotional/social development. When a child enters school, he enters a wider social world in which he must use his emotional resources and social skills to make a place for himself essentially on his own. Mother and father do not accompany him to school, and the teacher must divide her efforts among a roomful of children. When we think about the details of social living he must master, it is astounding how well and how fast he learns. Every day he meets, talks to, and relates to literally dozens of people with appropriate degrees of familiarity. He knows that he is not to speak to strangers, but recognizes that does not mean that he cannot ask a new clerk at the corner store for help. He figures out the authority chain of his school, determining who is the assistant janitor and who is the principal. He quickly distinguishes the sixth grader who is the safety patrol from the one who is the bully, and learns the appropriate response to each.

The middle-years child is not only learning social skills to help him in his current role—he is also learning about future roles. He is learning how to be a son, but also how to be a father. She is learning to read, but also learning to teach reading, a skill she may try out on a younger child in the family. Sometimes as parents we can get too concerned about teaching roles to our children. We should realize that the best thing we can do is offer warm encouragement as children learn and improve whatever skills they want to master.

The middle-years child is in the stage of *industry,* according to Stanford Eriksen's framework for development. He is a learner and a doer. The opposite of industry is *inferiority.* A child develops this feeling if he doesn't feel competent in the social and intellectual skills he is developing. You may need to help your child learn how to get along with his peers and adults so that he does not develop this feeling. What makes a child accepted socially? Studies have shown that even a popular name helps. But more important are such traits as friendliness and sociability, emotional control, energy applied to group-approved projects, intelligence and creativity (if not too much greater than that of the others), and sensitivity to others' moods and needs. For boys, athletic skills and physical size are important. Since most of these skills are to some extent learned—not innate—you can help your child develop them.

If his social/emotional development is proceeding well, he is learning the moral values of his family and his culture. He learns these by following examples of those he cares about, by receiving rewards and punishments, and by reasoning out good behaviors with others. These are the years when parents begin to worry about the effect other children's ideas have on the values their children are learning. The elementary school child does feel a strong need to conform because of peer pressure. This pressure steadily increases, as an interesting finding suggests: at age seven girls conform more than boys do, but by the end of the elementary school years both sexes are equally governed by conformity.

Apparently a small difference between the opinions of parents and peers helps the child define his own views and values. But the child is torn if there is a major difference between what his parents want and what his peers demand—e.g., if his parents oppose stealing but his peer group values skill in shoplifting. The child who can in these circumstances form and stick to moral convictions of his own is the one who has gotten a moderate to substantial amount of support and warmth at home, and who has been moderately disciplined and controlled by his parents. Under these conditions he seems to develop enough strength to resist social pressures and to make independent decisions about his lifestyle.

A social division typifies this age group: boys and girls in first grade show strong preference for their own sex, and seldom wish to be a member of the opposite sex. This preference tends to increase for several years, with boys becoming even more glad to be boys, and usually deciding that being a girl is really a bad break. Recent evidence suggests that this attitude is changing, that the sexes are more cooperative and friendly than they were a generation ago. This may be partly because the roles of men and women are changing—though we are still bound by them, as middle-years children prove. True, girls now have more freedom to choose activities they like—not just those designated "for women." But boys quite rigidly avoid behavior they have labeled "girlish." And by sixth grade the girls are beginning to lose their freedom and to fall into their traditional sex-assigned role. Unfortunately, as they do this they tend to underrate their own abilities and to overrate those of the boys.

Unlike the pre-school child, the middle-years child can greatly develop his ability to sympathize with and care for others. His new ability to think flexibly allows him to imagine himself in someone else's place. He needs frequent opportunities to do this with all types of people, both children and adults. Through these experiences he can develop a variety of solid friendships and good relationships. Adults who are close to him are his best source of information about the effect his actions have on others. If you have a child this age, express your feelings to him in a variety of situations, and encourage him to reciprocate.

The middle-years child also learns a great deal about social skills by playing games. As he plays by the rules, changes the rules with his friends, and pays the penalties of rule-breaking, he is learning to live with laws and regulations. Sometimes adults interfere too much in children's games. Naturally, you have to protect life and limb, but children can get much-needed practice in working out their own problems if they are left alone most of the time. Of course, if they seem ignorant or careless of the needs and rights of weaker or younger children, you will have to find ways to teach them concern. But remember that experiences which permit them to assume caring roles will help them much more than lectures will.

The emotional/social goals for the middle-years child are many. He should be aware of his own feelings and be able to control and use them suitably. He should also be concerned for the welfare of others and respond to other people's needs according to his resources and abilities. In addition, he should make friends in his peer group, and learn to feel competent and accepted socially; he should enjoy his family and draw emotional support from them. Besides developing his own morals and values, he should develop the strength to apply them in everyday life. He should also begin to define his adult role, and should have a variety of experiences to prepare him for assuming it.

Above all, growing up socially demands that the child increase his cooperative skills. He must learn to accept himself and others, to communicate effectively with others, and to work with others to create a social climate which is good for all. These goals are quite sophisticated—in fact, in many ways they can be lifetime goals.

Developmental Goals for the Teenager

I have changed the format slightly in this section. First I discuss the teenager's physical development, and then I discuss the other components of adolescence with the help of an outline developed by Dr. Donald W. Felker of Purdue University. This outline will help us see adolescence not as a problem period but as a time for a growing child to become increasingly mature.

Physical development. Adolescence is most easily defined as the period of the teenage years, although its physical starting point varies widely from child to child and from boy to girl. In boys the growth spurt which marks the beginning of physical adolescence begins between the ages of 10-1/2 and 16, the average age being 13. The growth rate peaks at about age 14, and slows down by 15; a boy may continue to grow slowly for several more years. In girls the growth spurt begins between the ages of 7-1/2 and 11-1/2; the average age is 11. Their growth rate peaks at about age 12 and slows to prespurt rate at about 13. Like boys, girls continue to grow for several more years.

Since many boys and girls don't know that it is perfectly normal for their individual growth rates to vary widely, an adult should make a point of telling them. The boy who is a late starter needs reassurance that his growth spurt is just a little late, that he will eventually catch up with his peers. The exceptionally tall sixth-grade girl needs to know that her friends will soon be growing fast, too. (In situations like these you might want to mention that a child who begins to grow later may end up being taller than most of his peers, because he will be slightly taller when his growth spurt begins.) An adolescent also needs to know that the first parts of the body to reach adult size are the head, the hands, and the feet. The ungainly look he may worry about will disappear as the rest of his body catches up.

The increase in height is accompanied by increased muscle growth and an increase in strength. This helps to explain the adolescent's growing interest in athletics, and the general physical restlessness that he often feels. Though he is no doubt healthy, the adolescent should have medical approval to participate in sports. Fortunately, most schools insist on physical examinations for all those students formally participating in sports programs, but parents should make certain that their teenager is physically able to compete in pickup games and informal competition.

Although the adolescent's body is growing rapidly, he weighs only about half as much as he will weigh as an adult. Yet the young adolescent already has a nearly adult-sized brain. One task of adolescence is to learn to use this well-developed gray matter!

One of the things weighing on the adolescent's mind is his sexual development. He tends to worry unnecessarily that he isn't keeping up with his peers. Remind him that, like height and growth rates, rates of sexual development vary greatly. Reassuring him that he is "normal" will help him accept himself. Give him accurate information, too. Tell a young girl that breast development, measured from the onset of the "bud stage," begins anywhere from age 8 to 13; reassure a young man that increase in testes size occurs anywhere from age 9-1/2 to 13-1/2.

If you're bringing an adolescent into your family, you are in a particularly trying position because you wonder what sexual information to give him. It is not easy to know how much the adolescent has learned prior to coming to live with you, or how accurate his information is. He may have been told that sex is shameful or dirty. Of course, it will be difficult for you to quickly establish the closeness you need to talk effectively about such an emotionally charged subject. But it is urgent that you provide—at the very least—clear, explicit written information that he can read for himself.

If you can't tell how much your teenager knows, it's best to follow the general rule that most teenagers need the most basic information about their own bodies. Even teenagers who appear highly sophisticated and sexually experienced often know very little about conception, pregnancy, venereal disease, and actual sexual functions. By providing such frank information you can help them develop the mature, healthy sexual attitudes that knowledge fosters. Do not be surprised or put off if the adolescent appears to be uninterested in the information. He may be unwilling to admit his lack of knowledge. Just make sure the information is good and readily available, and let his natural curiosity take its course. Ask your pastor, school counselor, or youth worker for suggestions for good reading materials, and make sure you read them yourself before you pass them on to the adolescent.

Nutrition also becomes exceptionally important in adolescence. This is a time when good eating habits tend to take a nose dive, yet a teenager's rapid growth and seemingly constant activity make a good diet essential. Nagging won't do much good, but regular mealtimes and well-planned meals may help to compensate for the "junk food" the teenager consumes. If a teenager's poor eating habits make him seriously overweight or underweight or cause other health problems, you should enlist the help of the teenager's doctor. Try to stay out of the picture yourself and let the doctor and the teenager manage the diet together. If this is not successful, ask the doctor to recommend the next step.

The teenager may devote a great deal of time and attention to his physical appearance. Within reasonable limits, I think it is best to let the adolescent assume responsibility for his personal hygiene, his clothing choices, his hairstyle, and other details of good grooming. In the next section I will discuss good grooming as a goal of adolescence.

Many teenagers worry particularly about skin problems—usually called acne. Though teenagers don't die of acne, I believe a trip to a dermatologist is very worthwhile for a teenager who is worrying about "zits." Perhaps he or she would be willing to share the expense with you. Treatment regimens suggested by dermatologists are often not much different from what you have been suggesting yourself ("wash better, cut those bangs, avoid everyday use of cosmetics"), but your willingness to take the problem seriously reassures the teenager. It is also easier for him to take advice from a doctor than from a parent.

In fact, the adolescent should see a doctor regularly—at least once every two years. If you have not already done so, this is a good time for you to fade out of the picture and let him handle making and keeping the appointment on his own. You can ask the doctor for a report later, if that's necessary. Remember that the adolescent should have regular dental checkups and eye examinations as well.

Sometimes an adolescent becomes quite preoccupied with his health, and often complains about physical problems. I think this may be partly because he no longer feels free to ask for the special attention and cuddling that a younger child might get, yet he wants some reassurance of his parents' love. Since he knows that a sick child usually gets more attention than a healthy child, the teenager might become "ill" to get this tender treatment. My husband and I have responded sympathetically and reassuringly when the teenagers in our home complained that they didn't feel well, and we discovered that their problems seldom lasted long. Even if you're sure that the teenager's problem isn't serious, it is sometimes worth the price of a doctor's examination to reassure the teenager of your continued concern and his own good health.

The goals for adolescent physical development challenge the teenager to become increasingly mature. He should have up-to-date, factual information about the physical/sexual changes he is undergoing, and he should be able to accept them without undue anxiety. On his own initiative he should be able to maintain good health habits. Within family guidelines he should assume responsibility for choosing, buying, and caring for his clothes, and otherwise managing his physical appearance. He should have regular examinations of his eyes, his teeth, and his general physical condition—checkups which he should be able to arrange himself.

Goals for Adolescents

I. Independence
A. Description: The child interacts principally with his parents to gain independence.

B. Characteristic abilities
1. Executive: the ability to carry out tasks
2. Volitional: the ability to think for oneself
3. Emotional: the ability to carry out ideas, to face challenges without becoming inappropriately emotional

II. Competence
A. Description: The child is guided principally by the school—teachers, other students—in gaining competence.

B. Characteristic abilities
1. Intellectual: the ability to reason
2. Vocational: the ability to support oneself
3. Social: the ability to behave maturely

III. Maturity
A. Description: The child becomes mature essentially on his own.

B. Characteristic growth
1. In self-evaluation: the child learns to accept himself.
2. In love: the child learns to love unselfishly.
3. In responsibility: the child learns to evaluate and accept responsibilities to other persons and institutions.
4. In values and goals: the child learns to establish adedequate personal goals and values.

Intellectual/emotional maturity. With the discussion of the adolescent's health and maturation as a backdrop, we can discuss the goals of adolescence listed in the preceding outline. The first of these goals is independence.

As he matures the adolescent becomes increasingly independent in every area of his life, though he begins this stage almost totally dependent on his family—particularly his parents. For example, when your son is twelve years old, you plan the meals, do the shopping, cook and serve meals at stated times, and keep track of his eating habits. Maybe he will help wash the dishes or take out the garbage. But at eighteen he might be living in two rooms with a buddy, and the two might on alternate weeks see that meals are served more or less regularly. Even this very simple illustration shows how the adolescent masters the basic components of independence: the executive ability to carry out tasks—to do such things as shopping or cooking; the volitional ability to choose—to have his own ideas about what he likes to eat; and the emotional ability to satisfy himself—to do something for himself and maintain his emotional equilibrium while doing it.

The parents are the primary people involved in the adolescent's transition from dependence to independence. They either grant him increasing freedom and responsibility, or they deny him the chance to grow up by keeping him dependent on them. Sometimes this happens unintentionally. It is helpful if parents remember that becoming independent is a process, not an act which happens all at once at a particular age.

Of course, certain responsibilities seem to be granted at certain ages—for example, letting the adolescent who has turned sixteen take out the car alone at night. How we as parents handle this situation can illustrate whether we are encouraging or frustrating independence. Have we given him the chance to learn how to drive well enough to do this? Will we let him go even if we think the trip is unnecessary, realizing that our reluctance may have little to do with his ability to drive, or our desire to curtail unnecessary trips—and a lot to do with our desire to keep him home, where we know he's safe?

Parents can also use a situation like this to assess their teenager's maturity. Has he worked at learning how to drive and how to take care of the car? Has he been willing to evaluate his reasons for wanting the car this time? Did he create a big scene to try to get it?

As parents we have a tendency to overreact to a

teenager's lack of skills. But the fact that he can't do everything does not mean he can do nothing. We also have a tendency to send out contradicting messages—"Grow up!" one minute and "You're too young!" the next. What a teenager needs is gradually increased responsibilities carefully matched to his abilities. This assures him that you want him to increase his accomplishments and to enjoy more privileges.

Of course, it's hard to sense what a teenager is ready for even if you have cared for him from infancy, because his readiness seems to fluctuate daily. Your task is even harder if the teenager is a new family member. But be direct—try asking him about a particular responsibility he is eager to undertake. Frankly discuss your fears, your expectations, and your perception of his abilities. You may end up jointly agreeing that he is not ready for the responsibility yet, but then planning steps that will help prepare him for it. Remember that your adolescent does not want to fail and "make a fool of himself." Help him plan for success and anticipate it with him.

Besides underrating the teenager's ability, parents also tend to give him the dirty jobs and then use his failure to do them as an excuse to withhold privileges. No one likes to carry out garbage, and a fourteen-year-old is no better equipped to do it than an adult is. Agreeing to take turns with the garbage and giving the fourteen-year-old another more exciting task—like cooking a meal one night a week—would give him a chance to learn new skills as well as ease the workload for the meal maker.

To want our children to be independent does not mean we want them to adopt an attitude that says, "I'll do my own thing—I don't care what happens to you" attitude. The person who is truly independent is not detached: he forms meaningful attachments to others, when it is needed, and is aware of how much he cares about others and how much they care about him. Remember that when your adolescent becomes independent, the giving and receiving between you will become thoughtfully voluntary. Certainly that is a goal worth working toward.

The second principal goal of adolescence is competence. Like independence, it has three main components: intellectual competence, or the ability to reason; vocational competence, or the ability to be economically self-sufficient; and social competence, or the ability to function in society as an adult. Though an adolescent usually becomes independent by interacting with his parents and family, our society usually expects the school to teach him competence. It remains the parents' responsibility to keep track of how well their child is doing in school—a task many parents find increasingly difficult during the adolescent years. Particularly if their child is having problems, parents may be at a loss to know how to help. Fortunately, there are certain things parents can do to foster a good working relationship between their child and the school. (Most of these steps should actually be taken before a child becomes a teenager.)

1. Stress the value of education to your child. If he has come from a family in which school was unimportant, try to work with the school and his teacher(s) to ensure that his experiences at school are positive ones.

2. Keep your child in school regularly. Your insistence on attendance is an action that not only says "school is important," but also helps ensure that he doesn't miss important learning steps.

3. Work for school programs which meet the needs of all kinds of students. Not all students are college-bound; work to eliminate the stigma attached to so-called vocational programs.

4. Structure family life to encourage studying. You may need to stipulate hours when the TV is to be turned off, provide quiet places for studying, supply dictionaries and atlases, and arrange library trips.

5. Reward a child's good performance in school with the same enthusiasm you display over his outstanding athletic feats or his holding a paying job.

Parents may also need to deliberately supplement the school's vocational training program if their child is involved in it. Choosing a career is a very scary and confusing task, and schools can't give teenagers all of the preparation they need. In fact, it is difficult for schools to provide more than textbook descriptions of jobs. Right now the problem seems to be that we educate teenagers for unavailable jobs. What we need to do is help young people choose jobs that are not only challenging and interesting but *available*.

How can you help? You can always assist by helping your teenager hold down a part-time job. This can be a lot of trouble: it may interfere with sleeping in on Saturdays, family vacations, or the schedule for using the family car. But it is also worthwhile. It gives the teenager the satisfaction of actual job experience as well as valuable practice in handling money—how to spend it and when to save it. You might also want to supplement the school's efforts by doing your best to acquaint your teenager with a variety of jobs. Neighbors or other acquaintances may be able to let your teenager visit the offices or factories where they work so that he can discover what various jobs are actually like.

Naturally, learning to relate to our children as adult workers takes time—it is a complex business certainly beyond the scope of this chapter. The least we can do as parents is honestly to acknowledge that the rest of our community sees our children as adults, even if we don't. Home was probably the last place where any of us felt "grown-up"; we should try to keep our children from feeling the same way.

The third main goal of adolescence is maturity, which an adolescent gains mainly by himself—by examining, nurturing, and understanding his feelings. According to Dr. Felker's outline, an adolescent's maturity can be measured by his ability to evaluate and accept himself, his ability to love himself and others, his ability to determine and accept personal responsibility to other persons and institutions, and his ability to develop adequate goals and values for himself.

Independence, competence, and maturity are such complex and important attributes that they can only be touched on in the few pages here. Still, they are described thoroughly enough so that you should be able to tell if your teenager has a conspicuous lack in one of these areas. If he does, he will need help. If you don't know how to help, I suggest you talk with a pastor or counselor and get help for both the child and yourself. If this is not possible, try consulting books. (This book can give you helpful information about self-image, self-evaluation, and values and goals.) Remember, too, that the adolescent can't grow up overnight. Be patient. As a mature, concerned adult you can be an important role model for your teenager, and can help him overcome his immaturity if you are willing to work with him.

In communities across the nation, child welfare agencies have great difficulty finding good homes for adolescents. I think this may be an indication that psychologists and others have made parents unnecessarily anxious about the adolescent years. They are challenging years, certainly—but they are also very rewarding ones. Enjoy your teenager for the individual he is, and let him enjoy you. He will soon be on his way to adulthood.

A Child's Spiritual Development

In the above summaries I have not discussed the very important subject of spiritual development. But I planned this omission purposely because spiritual development defies categories and stages—it is highly individual and cannot be charted and predicted in a definite way. It needs to be discussed in a less structured way, something I will try to do here.

We should first of all consider some basic assumptions about the child as a spiritual being—assumptions that will help us appropriately guide our child's spiritual development.

We assume that the child is a person in his own right and, as such, the equal of his parents in value. A child is not a second-class citizen; his soul is of the same infinite worth.

We assume that children need the help of adults to grow up well. They are not blank slates on which adults may write anything they please; they are not flowers that will blossom regardless of nurturing. Rather, each child is a person in process who needs careful guidance and ample affection. Without loving supervision, he is too inclined to want his own way; ignorant of his own potential for good; unaware of the consequences of his own behavior.

We assume that the parent is not the owner of the child, but a guardian responsible to God for the complete and devoted care of him. The parent is to be concerned with the child's total well-being—spiritual, mental, emotional, and physical.

We assume that God has made available to parents the resources they need to parent children well. He has given and will continue to give us skill, insight, and knowledge, and He will provide the grace we need to nurture them daily—for their good and to His glory.

We assume that, as a moral being, the child is sinful. This means that he will need the redemptive grace of God in his personal life, and that he will need guidance to grow toward God and to learn how to live for Him.

A parent has three distinguishable tasks to perform in guiding his child's spiritual development. Because they are interrelated, separation is slightly inappropriate, but it makes discussion easier.

Certainly the most obvious task is helping the child appreciate and adopt religious practices. In order to begin to understand the significance of these practices, a child needs opportunities to experience them and participate in them. When you add a child to your family, remember that his religious beliefs and practices may be very different from yours. If this is the case, you will want to respect his beliefs, yet encourage him to worship with your family. Or your new child may have no strong religious background at all. In both of these situations, you will need to help the child feel welcome in the religious circle of your family life. If he needs some basic instruction in religious practices, help him tactfully and thoughtfully.

For example, if you are going to take your child to religious services, stop to consider what information he may need about public worship. Does he know the kind of conduct expected in a church? Does he know the expected courtesies? Make sure you explain to him even the small details of these activities; if you don't, he may feel awkward and out of place.

When I was young, my brothers and sisters and I often "played church": all of us took turns at playing the roles we considered the most interesting or the most important. If you have young children, why not let them try this: let them take turns being the organist, the deacon, the minister. Be especially careful to prepare the adolescent for basic church rituals. For example, if the Sunday School class that he will join frequently looks up Bible verses and reads them aloud, make sure he knows how to do this, or speak to his teacher ahead of time. Remember that many adolescents do not know how to look up a Bible verse. Others are not used to reading aloud, and might be embarrassed to do so. Be sure you know what your child is likely to encounter, and try to prepare him for it. If he is reluctant to attend church or Sunday School, remember that he may really be embarrassed or afraid.

Religious education is a natural extension of these religious practices. Remember that you are responsible for a child's religious education while he is a member of your family. Exactly what kind of school the child will attend is an issue that you should discuss with his biological parents before he comes to live with you. If a child is already living with you and you haven't done this, you may need to settle this issue now. Keep in mind that your uncertainty on this matter can hurt the child. If you and his biological parents continually disagree about his training, he may avoid committing himself to any of the values he is being taught—and he may eventually reject what you want him to learn.

You also need to consider your child's background when you teach him personal devotions. My husband and I have discovered that young children with no previous religious training love to join in family worship if they are taught short, simple songs and prayers, and if Bible readings and stories are geared to their attention span. They also rapidly accept bedtime prayers as one of the important parts of their nightly ritual. Predictably, older children are less easily persuaded to adopt these practices. When dealing with them, provide suggestions and guidelines, but allow them some freedom and flexibility, some opportunity to individualize their spiritual behavior. Be adaptive, be thoughtful, and pray for good results in the life of your family.

Remember that you should also introduce your child to religious history, art, and music—and remember that the school system does not emphasize these subjects as strongly as it once did. Aside from their religious value, these subjects are culturally significant. A child is a cultural orphan in western society if he is not aware of the influence of Jewish and Christian religion on all aspects of our civilization.

For this reason, take him to museums, to concerts, and help him visit other churches—perhaps at a time when they are sponsoring an event open to the community. Activities like this can help teach a child respect and appreciation for the religious beliefs and practices of others. He needs to learn that he can cherish his own beliefs without scorning and belittling those of others. Particularly with younger children, try using games and puzzle books (available at your local religious bookstore) to teach them facts about a variety of religions. Almost all children will enjoy these games if interested, caring adults will join in playing them.

The second task of spiritual development is teaching the child to apply what he believes to his daily moral behavior. Lawrence Kohlberg and others have studied moral development and have attempted to specify how and when moral development takes place. Actually, it seems to be sequential, just like cognitive development: the child learns to operate at a simple level, then learns to operate on a more sophisticated level. His moral development is directly related to his ability to master moral decision-making, which is made up of two elements—content and motivators. This simply means that the child must learn both the what and the why before he is able to make moral decisions. For example, he must learn *the fact* that stealing is wrong, and he must learn a reason *why* that will motivate him not to steal. The apprehension of this dual process is gradual, and learning the fact precedes understanding the why. The young child may make a decision not to take a cookie because Mother said it is stealing, which is bad, and because Mother will punish him if he does. An older child might make that same decision, but on the basis that stealing is wrong because it deprives other people of their belongings, and because he will feel guilty—a much more sophisticated behavioral response.

Because it is partly based on knowledge and partly based on motivation, moral development does not proceed automatically. Your new child may be very knowledgeable in most areas, but may have been inadequately taught (either by word or example) about what is right or wrong. He may, for instance, lie easily, frequently, and apparently without guilt.

This behavior might also reflect a lack of motivation. Remember that a child's conscience develops out of his attachment to a parental figure. If your child has not felt he belonged to someone, or if he has been shuttled from adult to adult, he may need time to become attached to you and form the internal controls we call conscience. His level of maturity, his previous experiences, and his relationships with people—all of these factors will affect his ability to make moral decisions and to honor them.

Actually, very few children under twenty are able to see reasons behind laws, to internalize principles, and to establish priorities among principles. But parents must encourage this development by thinking and talking in these terms, and by letting their children know that they make moral decisions by considering these factors. Specifically, you can encourage your child's moral development in the following ways:

1. Give reasons for your rules. Explain them, and explain the rationale behind them.
2. Use some family worship times to tell stories that illustrate moral dilemmas and problems. Then give your children opportunities to suggest and discuss solutions to the problems you present.
3. Introduce your child to a variety of other children so that he can learn to positively assert what he believes—at a time when you are there to support and encourage him. For example, if there is a child in your neighborhood who has a bad influence on your child, give the two of them an opportunity to play together under your supervision, so that you can guide their interaction.
4. Encourage the child to belong to your family in every way—spiritually, emotionally, etc. (Suggestions for doing so are found throughout the book.) If he feels he belongs to you, he will want to be like you—in spiritual and other important ways.

You may want to visit your local library for more materials on moral development and the growth of conscience. Look under the headings "attachment," "identification," and "moral development."

The third task of spiritual development is encouraging

your child to form a personal spiritual identity—the most challenging and significant kind of development, and the most difficult to discuss. Spiritual development is incomplete if the child goes through the motions of moral and religious behavior but lacks a personal spiritual identity. He needs to know God in an intimate and individual way. Parents cannot force this kind of development; only the Holy Spirit can make the child spiritually alive and bring him to personally know and accept God. But there is still much we can do as parents. We can demonstrate by the way we live and the way we nurture our families that God is real to us. And we can be sure that we conscientiously and prayerfully teach the child, by instruction and example, how to worship meaningfully and behave morally, realizing that these behaviors usually form the basis for the child's personal spiritual commitment. Certainly leading a child to God in these ways can be the greatest reward—and the greatest responsibility—that a parent can have.

CHAPTER 3

USING DISCIPLINE
EFFECTIVELY

Discipline is a much talked-about subject. Parents are deluged with advice: library shelves and bookstore racks are crammed with articles and books on the subject. I am not going to try to summarize or repeat information that is readily available elsewhere. But I do want to explain how discipline in the restructured family differs from that in a more typical family, and what particular problems and goals that family has. In this chapter I will outline some principles of good discipline and try to relate them to the special needs of your family.

What do we mean when we use the word *discipline?* I'm sure you have heard someone launch an attack on teenagers and finish by saying, "The trouble with kids today is they just don't get enough discipline." We suspect he means physical punishment when he says "discipline." We do not mean the same thing when we say, "His teacher just doesn't have good discipline in the classroom." We probably mean yet another thing when we say, "I want my children to be able to discipline themselves." When I use the word *discipline* in this book, I am referring to all of the methods we use to train a child to meet standards that satisfy both his needs and those of other people.

What Is Good Discipline?

Good discipline benefits the child. Guiding our treatment of our children must be a deep-seated, genuine concern that what we do will promote the child's good. We cannot be hard on a child or force him into a mold if it will not help him in the long run. Of course ideas about good discipline vary, but good motives must always be a factor. And we must take particular care that our actions reflect our good intentions.

Good discipline benefits the entire family. In schools, teachers sometimes call the classroom a "climate for learning"; something similar can be said of a family. And just as a rebellious child upsets the climate of a classroom, a rebellious teenager upsets the climate of the family. Generally speaking, one unhappy or unruly family member negatively affects the whole family; one happy or "improving" family member positively influences it. When we discipline one child, then, we have to consider how it will affect other family members. I remember the time when my husband and I were getting after one child about his schoolwork. Ironically, he didn't seem to be much affected by our urging—but our first grader became very intense and uncertain about her schoolwork, and ended up bursting into tears in her classroom over a less-than-perfect paper.

Good discipline stresses the present. A caring parent naturally has set long-term goals for his child that affect his daily actions. The danger is letting future goals interfere with today's discipline. The primary reason we want a four-year-old to eat a good dinner is not that we want him to grow up big and strong like Daddy, but that he needs the energy and nutrition from that food *today* to be a healthy and energetic four-year-old. Remember, too, that a child—particularly a younger child—understands short-term goals better than long-term ones. If you stress the short-term benefits of a particular action, a child will be more likely to discipline himself to perform it.

Good discipline is suited to the child's age. This may seem quite obvious. Of course we can't pick up a screaming teenager like we might an overwrought two-year-old and carry him to his room to settle down. But it's not as easy to notice that we are talking down to our fifteen-year-old because of the tone of voice we are using, or that we are restricting the freedom of a twelve-year-old as though he were still a first grader. Because the child is constantly growing and maturing, we must constantly adapt our discipline to his level of maturity.

Good discipline gives a child freedom. The object of good discipline is not to keep the child imprisoned in a safe place, but to set him on a good road and teach him to avoid the dangers on the way. When the child knows what you expect, what the difficulties are, and what the goal is, he feels free to pursue that goal using his unique methods and abilities. A child who does not know what you want or what trouble spots to anticipate will constantly challenge you and test situations, wasting a lot of emotional energy on what may seem to him a hopeless task. He doesn't know what to expect in general or what you expect in particular.

The older child who joins your family may have a particularly hard time because of the transition he must make: he moves from the clearly defined limits set by his family to the unknown limits of your family. He will probably test you quite a bit to discover what those limits are—and you should establish them plainly and firmly. People who work with severely delinquent children believe that even they respond best to clear limits when they are fairly and lovingly enforced in ways that preserve the child's dignity.

Good discipline reinforces your family's goals and values. Discipline does not exist apart from the goals you set for your family. When you decide that you value education, or set a goal that each child will develop a skill to make him economically self-supporting by age twenty-one, the value or goal must be reinforced by your discipline. You must establish appropriate rules about finishing homework and earning weekly allowances. Good discipline does not interfere with accomplishing family goals and does not conflict with family values. Have you ever wondered why in some school districts the penalty for skipping school is suspension from classes? I have, but I recognize too that as a parent I sometimes set the same kind of trap for myself. What will a child think if the punishment for biting another child is that you will bite him? Let me give another, more complicated example. The parents decide to give their children allowances to teach them how to handle money responsibly. But then the parents take away the five-year-old's allowance for a week to punish him for fighting with his sister. This punishment, which attempts to enforce one value (getting along in the family), tends to interfere with the other value (learning to handle money responsibly). It establishes a third contradictory value: money is a weapon for punishment. We can't avoid all such instances, but we should guard against our good intentions going awry in our disciplinary patterns.

Good discipline builds the child's self-control. A parent is in some senses a person who is vigorously working himself out of a job—and this is especially true of him as a disciplinarian. The goal of good discipline is that day when the child is able to responsibly manage his own life. His conscience guides him, his will restrains his impulses, and his plans structure his work. This is not an overnight occurrence, although the goal of good discipline is to daily increase the child's personal responsibility, to let him make choices and accept the consequences of his actions. The good disciplinarian relinquishes his authority and control as he trusts and encourages the child to assume responsibility. Sometimes it seems we take two steps forward and one step back, but the important thing is that we are always struggling to move ahead.

Good discipline is designed to prevent rather than cure misbehavior. Instead of stocking a drugstore of medicine to cure illnesses, careful parents try to keep their child well. Similarly, good parents try to spend their time encouraging their child to behave well rather than devising remedies for poor behavior. Of course, preventive medicine can't eliminate all illnesses or all misbehavior—but it helps.

Why Does He Misbehave?

Now let's take a look at some of the causes of misbehavior. We should start by reminding ourselves that any kind of behavior has multiple causes that are interrelated and complex. For this reason, pinpointing the "why" of behavior is never entirely possible. But we can make some intelligent guesses about what triggers misbehavior, and learn to minimize or eliminate those causes. Following is a listing of the most probable causes.

Let's start with a very simple explanation for misbehavior:

1. *The child didn't know the action was wrong.* This is a distinct possibility when a child has recently joined his functional family. What seems very obvious to you with your background may not be at all clear to him. Be sure he understands not only your rules but your explanation of them. Remember that his vocabulary may be different from yours.

2. *Something is wrong with the child physically.* He may be sick, tired, upset, hungry, or in some other way physically unable to react as you wanted him to.

3. *The child is getting too many conflicting signals.* This can be a particular problem in restructured families. The child is confused because of the inconsistency between school rules, home rules, rules when he visits his married sister, and so forth. So many different people and environments are placing demands on him that he doesn't know how to behave. He probably can't express his feelings, so you may have to discern his problem and talk it over with him. Manners might be a problem. For instance: At home you all eat at the table together, and good manners are taught and enforced; in the school lunchroom everyone bolts his food and hurries outside; at his sister's home there are no regular meals, and he is expected to grab a sandwich when he is hungry and eat it anywhere. So manners appropriate in the lunchroom are considered rude at home. If such discrepancies are occasional, the child can probably handle them, but if they occur frequently the child will probably get confused and misbehave because he is disoriented.

4. *There is a conflict of values in the home.* Various parent figures, a grandmother, an older sister, or other adults in the home may be stressing different values and rules. Consistency within the family can eliminate this problem.

5. *Too much outside influence.* This problem is related to number four above, and can particularly plague a functional family. In this case people outside the child's family contra-

dict—sometimes deliberately—what people in his family tell him. The result, of course, is confusion.

6. *He is testing the disciplinary limits of your family* (an idea mentioned previously). Every child has a way of finding out what is acceptable and what isn't in a particular environment. If a child has recently joined your family and is facing a new situation, he may misbehave or he may simply be misjudging what is appropriate behavior in your family. In either case, the child is not necessarily consciously aware of what he is doing.

7. *The parents are following the swing of the pendulum too much.* Parents are constantly flooded with advice from all kinds of sources. Most parents let the bulk of it roll off their backs and continue to manage their family according to established patterns. But occasionally a very conscientious parent becomes too impressed with "expert advice" and begins to follow it too closely. Since popular "expert advice" changes much like a pendulum swings, the parent devoted to it may use "Method A" for child-rearing only to switch to "Method B" when it becomes popular. Obviously a child can't keep up with such frequent and substantial changes.

8. *The child is living up to his label of "behavior problem."* I think this is particularly a problem in functional families. A young girl joining a family may have poor school and community records, and may misbehave often. Under these circumstances her new family and others might label her a "bad girl"; ironically, she may *continue* to behave badly to live up to these expectations. She may even have learned to identify herself in negative terms: "I'm a trouble-maker" or "I'm no good." Remember that children usually blame themselves for the dissolution of their family *regardless of the real reason* for it, and this blame may reinforce their belief that they're "bad."

9. *The child feels insecure.* I am not referring to the "nobody loves me" kind of insecurity, but rather to the insecurity that develops when standards are too high or too low. In the former case the child may ask himself, "Will I ever be able to measure up? Probably not." In the latter case he will say to himself, "Nobody thinks I'm capable of anything." And in either case he will think, "I might as well quit trying."

10. *The child is imitating the bad behavior of others.* TV and other mass media, friends, neighborhood gangs, and other

outside influences may provide poor models that encourage him to misbehave.

11. *He is sending you a message which you will have to decipher.* For instance: If you have seemed indecisive about what you want from him, the message of his bad behavior may be, "Hey, set some limits." Or the message may be, "Leave me alone." Especially in a new relationship, the intense or frequent ways in which you try to show you care may be too much for a child. He may want some privacy to adjust to what is happening. Try to be available, but don't overwhelm him with constant attention. A boy in his middle teens seems most sensitive about his privacy; unfortunately, if his parents don't understand his need to withdraw and think things through, they may intrude with too much well-intentioned advice and guidance.

12. *You are using too many kinds of disciplinary methods.* That is, you are reacting to a particular behavior consistently, but you are doing it in too many different ways. The first time he hits his sister you try isolation; when he does it again, you threaten and scold; the next time you forbid him to watch TV. When that doesn't work you switch techniques and try bribery. But the misbehavior continues—possibly because your child is encouraged by your inconsistency. He misbehaves because he doesn't mind some of the punishments very much and considers them a low enough price to pay for the misbehavior.

13. *The child thinks that the parents are playing favorites.* This favoritism may be real or imagined. Whatever its type it causes much disobedience—disobedience not always attributed to the right child. A common problem in restructured families, favoritism requires careful handling. (I will discuss favoritism more thoroughly in the section about fighting and rivalry in Chapter 5.)

14. *The environment is too complicated for the child.* Particularly if he is away from home, a child may misbehave because a situation is foreign to him or is not geared to his needs. Consider a laundromat, the checkout aisle of a grocery store, a large, busy department store, or an adult church service—children frequently misbehave in these environments. Remember that environments which your other chil-

dren have learned to handle (such as that adult church service) may be unfamiliar and complicated to your new child.

15. *The child is trying to get attention.* This may seem like an overworked explanation for bad behavior, but it's not an easy one. Once you've decided that this is the problem, you still need to figure out what kind of attention he wants, and why. You also need to decide if that attention will be good for him.

How to Eliminate Causes of Misbehavior

Now that we have looked at some of the causes of misbehavior, what are some ways we can eliminate them? Some corrective measures probably occurred to you as you read the previous section. Others you have been using for years, perhaps without realizing it. Now you need to consciously apply your methods to this child who is misbehaving. Here are some ideas I have tried successfully.

Improve the child's physical condition. The chapter on goals and development suggests the relationship between health and behavior. In fact, misbehavior may be linked to specific physical problems such as hearing loss, or to general problems like poor nutrition. Both kinds can be improved or corrected. The handicapped or chronically ill child may present special discipline problems; ask your school counselor or doctor to recommend reading material on the subject.

Restructure the day. Add or take away a nap, change bedtime, schedule more outdoor play, be sure meals are served regularly, add a snack if he needs energy between meals. If a child seems to misbehave at certain times, such as the times when you are trying to make supper or help an older child with homework, make some changes in how to handle that part of the day. Experiment, but try each new system long enough to give it a chance to prove or disprove itself.

Restructuring is important for older as well as younger children. Perhaps you invariably fight with your young teenager if you ask for a little help with chores right after he gets home from school. If you try to think through the situation, you realize that he is in a fairly strict environment all day at his junior high: many adults are telling him what to do and he has little freedom of choice. He gets out of school and returns to the freedom of home only to have you—another adult—tell him what to do. Because you act as a trigger, he takes out all of his pent-up frustrations on you, and you don't like it.

You can stick with your pattern and fight with your son day after day for months. Or you can decide to talk to him and say something like this: "John, I realize that all day long people are telling you what to do. I appreciate the fact that you do what is required and have a reputation for handling yourself well at school. I need to ask you to do some things, too, but I guess my timing has been pretty poor. I thought we might try something different. Maybe I should postpone reminding you about the chores. Or maybe we should just agree that you'll do them, and I'll try to stay out of the when and how. Or maybe you have some ideas about how we could avoid yelling at each other every day." Together you set up a structure that doesn't trigger the misbehavior. You both feel better, the chores are getting done—and you are teaching him a constructive way to handle conflict.

Learn to listen. As I said before, I think "He's trying to get attention" is a somewhat overworked explanation for misbehavior. But it is quite possible for us to get so involved in our own thoughts or activities that we just don't hear what is going on. The child begins to play with the dishes in the sink; but we go on talking to a neighbor. We "come to" only when there is a crash and a favorite vase lies shattered on the floor. It is especially important to remain aware of what a small child is doing, because his physical safety may often be at stake. But you also need to listen carefully to the older child, who may drop verbal hints about what he plans to do. If you don't respond clearly, he may assume that he has your consent. In fact, he may ask your permission for things when he *knows* you're distracted, hoping for a vague "I guess so" instead of a "no." But if you often say "Umm" instead of really responding, you have only yourself to blame when the family car is suddenly missing. Fortunately, parents today can take methods courses to learn how to listen effectively to their children. You might enjoy taking one of these courses yourself.

Look for bad patterns and interrupt them. Not long ago I noticed that there was invariably fighting if another eight-year-old joined our eight-year-old and five-year-old in the basement. One of the three always ended up crying. But this didn't happen when the playmate was another younger child. Since the visit only happened once a week, I decided to be pragmatic: I played with the five-year-old while the eight-year-olds played by themselves. I just didn't have the time to teach this "occasional trio" how to play together—particularly since the playmate varied from week to week. If an eight-year-old had been coming every day, or if the same child had been coming every week, I probably *would* have worked with the trio. You probably have trouble patterns at your house, too. Maybe a fight is triggered by a particular TV show one child wants to watch each week. And maybe Dad's homecoming seems to set off the trouble. Look for bad patterns like this and devise practical ways to disrupt them.

Be flexible. Individualize your responses. If being a parent were simply a matter of making a set of rules and enforcing them, we could turn over the rearing of children to a robot. But it isn't that simple; a good parent knows that there are times when he must make exceptions to his own rules. Some parents fear that this flexibility will make them look like "soft touches," and will encourage their children to wheedle and whine to get their own way. I don't think this will happen. If your child knows that you do sometimes make exceptions for good reason, he will be encouraged to request an exception in an adult way, presenting a careful rationale for his request. Recently our thirteen-year-old asked for an exception to the family rule against staying overnight with friends on Saturday night. Her "case" was logical, so we made the exception. Since that time she has been even more responsible about getting to bed early on Saturday night and getting up on time for church, though we did not spell this out as a condition of her going. Because we grant meaningful exceptions, she accepts the rule and is more inclined to obey it.

Children also want us to treat them as individuals. We frequently expect children to be different than their peer group pressures them to be. In return we should be willing to treat them as persons, not as a group. At times this is very difficult in the functional family. Perhaps you trust only one of your two teenagers to drive the family car safely. It is not really fair to deny the privilege to one until the other has earned it. It is better to talk directly and privately to each young person about the reasons for your decision. Of course, it is easier to hide behind rules like, "No kids in this family can drive a car until they finish high school." But they usually create only ill will, not harmony. Agencies frequently establish such general rules for foster children in placement homes, and the children resent them deeply.

Be consistent and make your expectations clear. Making exceptions is not possible unless the rule is clear in the first place. Last winter I was in an adult group in which we were discussing family rules that had prevailed in the homes in which we had grown up. They were things like, "If you can't say something nice, say nothing at all" and "If you must wrestle, go outside." One woman remarked that there was clearly a rule in her childhood home that said, "We don't slam doors!" She had always obeyed it and was enforcing it in her present home—yet she could not remember ever being *told* not to slam doors. This is the kind of rule that can give families the most trouble: the kind that is assumed but never spelled out.

In the restructured family, unspoken rules may be unknown rules. The child joining you may have come from a family that went by the rule, "If you have something to say, say it!" But in your family the rule is, "Don't speak until you are calm enough to talk reasonably." His shouting at you may obey his family's rule about bluntness, but it doesn't satisfy your rule about calm communication, and you may react to it as deliberate misbehavior. Maybe in your family it carries a negative label like "talking back." Naturally you have the right to expect a new child to adapt to the rules of your family, but

you will need to be sure he knows them first. You will no
doubt try to learn his family's rules, too. In fact, you and the
child may need to make some of the same adjustments that
two adults make when they marry and weave their different
family backgrounds into a new pattern for the family they will
have.

Consistency is not the same as inflexibility. Rules must
sometimes bend for individual personalities, and be subject to
spontaneous change. Consistency means, however, that you
will not insist that a child clean every morsel from his plate
one meal, then look the other way when he scrapes it into the
dog's dish the next. You will try to keep the promises you
make and follow through on your commitments.

Discuss your rules. Be willing to discuss behavior and
rules at times when all of you are calm enough to listen. Make
explanations, give reasons, listen to your children's suggestions. We have the beautiful gift of language; let's use it to improve family life. Remember that even very young children
understand more words than they can use. I am not saying
that you must always be able to convince your children of the
validity of your rules. They may not yet be able to understand your reasons. If you have done your best to explain a
rule and the child is still reluctant to obey it, it doesn't hurt to
say, "Do it because I'm the mother in this house and I say so."
Note the phrasing. Don't say, "Because I'm your mother," if
the child can mentally retort, "No, you're not." Rely on the
role of the parent instead of a biological claim. The child
knows that you, as one of the heads of the family, have final
say in the decision.

Don't make everything a major issue. Keep things in perspective, and sort out what is really important and what is not.
A battle over hair length may disguise a disagreement over a
more important issue; debate that issue instead of getting into
a silly argument about surface appearances. Maintain a sense
of humor. Don't be afraid to admit you were wrong, to apolo-
gize. Your child is probably going to make it—our parents
worried about us, and we did.

How to Respond to Behavior—
Good and Bad

We have discussed misbehavior quite thoroughly—what causes it and how to eliminate it. But what about those bad behavior patterns that seem so hard to break? How can we handle them in ways that will help the child learn to control himself?

Let's back up and talk about the different ways we react to good behavior and bad behavior. This is what we usually do.

- We often ignore good behavior: we expect it and don't think it calls for any special notice. After all, the child is only doing what he should be doing.

- Sometimes we reward good behavior. This is less common than taking it for granted, but most parents are in the habit of noticing and praising or otherwise rewarding some of their child's good behavior.

- Occasionally we actually punish good behavior—because we think we are punishing bad behavior. If, for example, the child is helping us wash the dishes and he breaks a cup, we might scold him. We think we are punishing him for being careless, but the child feels he is being punished for trying to help. We tend to respond to bad behavior in a reverse pattern.

- We usually attempt to punish bad behavior.

- We sometimes reward bad behavior—not intentionally of course. The child wanted something from us and got it, but we didn't intend for it to work out that way. For instance: while you are talking with your sister your eight-year-old repeatedly does something to torment the cat. When polite asides to him to stop don't work, you finally interrupt yourself to give him a severe warning. Your sister doesn't want to witness a family discipline problem, so she goes home. Now your son has you to himself and can talk about his day at school, which is what he wanted in the first place.

- We sometimes ignore bad behavior. We do this because some experts have told us that ignoring bad behavior makes it go away. Actually I don't think this works well in families. If the behavior registers at all with us—which it must do if we have labeled it "bad"—we will find a way to respond to it sooner or later. I have steadfastly ignored bad behavior for half an hour—or thought I did—and then have used that same behavior as a reason to punish a child when my patience ran out. I was not ignoring it at all, but was silently letting my disapproval of it build until I reached my breaking point.

In short, we have learned that we should encourage and reward good behavior. We also know that we should discourage bad behavior—we try ignoring it, refusing to reward it, and punishing it. Any parent will agree with this two-sentence theory, and will also agree that it is not so easy to carry out as it sounds. It may be particularly difficult to follow this theory with the child who has just joined the family. Here are some of the problems commonly encountered.

Parents ask, "If I reward good behavior, won't he always expect a reward? I want him to do the right thing because it is right." Naturally we will not notice and reward all of a child's good behavior: we don't have time to devote ourselves so completely to him. In any case the child will be doing the right thing most of the time without our even noticing. And isn't it true that "virtue is its own reward?" C. S. Lewis deals with that question in a way that is helpful to me. He suggests that this is just another way of saying that rewards should be natural to the situation. He uses this illustration: If a man loves a woman and succeeds in making her his wife, we think he has won the natural reward of his love. On the other hand, if a shrewd father pays him to marry a woman he does not love, we regard him as a cold-hearted materialist. In other words, we see a wife as the natural reward of loving, not an object to barter with. The parallel? We should try to make the reward fit the situation, to make it part of the natural outcome of doing the thing required; this allows less room for manipulation. A compliment to a child on a job well done is a natural reward that can become part of the job's satisfaction. A young girl who is learning to take good care of her clothes can be "naturally" rewarded with a new dress.

Always supplement a material reward with a word of

praise or appreciation and maybe a hug. At first it may take a piece of candy and praise to get the job done; later the commendation alone, plus the child's own good feeling about himself, will be ample reward. Eventually the child will learn to work without notice most of the time—though I have never known anyone, adult or child, who didn't appreciate a word of thanks.

Parents sometimes say that rewarding good behavior is difficult because they don't have time to constantly watch for it. I'm a parent, too, and I know this is a difficult problem. You have more things to attend to than one child's behavior. What you might do is compromise: if you can't notice everything, decide to notice *something*. Decide what particular behavior is important to you, and then concentrate on noticing and rewarding it. It really isn't necessary to reward everything. You should also ask yourself if you usually notice only bad behavior. It is the ratio of praise to blame, or success to failure, that is important. If you discover that you must correct a child often, it is even more important that you praise his good behavior so that he won't get discouraged about himself or his ability to please you.

Parents also have a hard time ignoring bad behavior. Probably the most common response is, "I tried ignoring it and it didn't work." Some of you are probably like me; you notice bad behavior and don't comment on it at the time, but you don't really ignore it—in fact, you respond to it sooner or later. In laboratory tests, ignored behavior does go away. But a home is not a laboratory, and families don't operate like experimental rooms. It also might be impractical to ignore certain kinds of behavior. But if you can do it, it will work.

Perhaps the problem is that you freely admit you do not want to ignore bad behavior. The behavior bothers you, and you believe you should do something about it right away. If you must react, at least try to plan your reaction. Explore your options, making sure that you don't somehow reward the behavior, and that the punishment you choose is consistent with your goal.

Some parents feel they cannot ignore misbehavior because it is their duty to teach their child justice by punishing *all* bad behavior. I call this the "Job's friends" approach. Job's friends believed that there is or should be an absolute correlation between wrongdoing and punishment. With our limited wisdom and capacity to understand, this just isn't possible. At best our justice is mixed. We cannot punish to keep the scales of justice balanced. Our goal is good behavior; if ignoring bad behavior makes it stop, we should attempt to ignore it. Ignoring a child's behavior does not mean we are unaware of it; it simply means we have made a conscious decision not to respond to it. Nor does ignoring indicate approval, indifference, or laziness. It is meant to be a positive tool for discouraging misbehavior.

What Is Effective Punishment?

Those who have studied the relationship between discipline and behavior have concluded that the most effective way to change and guide behavior is to reward good behavior and to sometimes ignore bad behavior, sometimes punish it. Since punishment is widely used, I want to offer some guidelines and cautions. I'll start with the cautions.

Punishment is dangerous! It is dangerous because it sometimes gives us an excuse to behave badly ourselves. We can be guilty of trying to get even; of giving in to bitterness, which simply breeds a responsive bitterness in the child; or of exploiting authority. Not even parents have absolute authority.

Punishment is also dangerous because it does work—but often only temporarily. It can very effectively suppress bad behavior, tricking us into thinking that the problem is settled when it is not. The child may simply disguise the misbehavior, or he may become hostile.

Another danger of punishment is alienation: it can cause the child to avoid us. We turn away from things that hurt us in some way, yet we want the child to turn to us for love and help even though we realize that our punishment sometimes wounds him. Of course punishment is sometimes necessary, but we must be careful that we don't drive the child away with it.

Perhaps the most serious flaw of punishment is that it does not provide a model for good behavior. It may stop bad behavior, but punishment alone is never enough to encourage good alternative behavior. It needs to be used with another behavioral method to succeed at that.

Nevertheless, punishment *can* be used effectively. Following are some guidelines.

1. Punishment should be administered only by those directly involved in teaching the child. This is logical enough, because punishment is a teaching method, a means of instruction. In the home, punishment usually should be administered by the family's "teachers"—the parents. My husband and I have older children who help a great deal with the younger ones, but as a rule they do not administer punishment except at those times when a parent isn't present and punishment is genuinely necessary. That is, they might scold a child for leaving the yard, or make him sit on a chair for a few minutes for violating a safety rule. We have also made it clear to these older children that they can administer only certain kinds of punishment. This matter of who can punish and how ought to be clearly spelled out in a functional family.

2. Punishment should always be motivated by love. I am not talking about a sticky kind of emotion, but about a genuine commitment of the heart and will to the child's welfare. He should not be punished because he made you look bad, or because your mother expects it, or for any other reason besides your concern for his well-being.

3. Punishment should have limited and specific goals. Let me illustrate. My eight-year-old comes home from school and throws his coat on the kitchen floor by the door. I notice and say pleasantly, "Please hang up your coat." He ignores me. If this has been a day-after-day problem, my next response may be to punish him in some way. My justification for it might be something like, "That kid has to learn that when I say something I mean business." So I decide to cancel his after-school playtime and to give him an extra chore. Yes, he does need to learn that I mean business; it is one of my general goals. But the punishment will be more effective if I am more specific— if I say to him, "You have to learn to hang up your coat when I ask you to do it." Of course my general goal is important, but the child will respond better to specific cues, and both of us can more clearly see his progress in obedience if I am exact about my expectations. The next day when he comes home from school and does hang up his coat, I can say, "Thanks for hanging up your coat today." He is encouraged and I am encouraged. Maybe it isn't a very big step, but it is positive and measurable, and it is consistent with the general goal I am working toward in many different ways.

4. *Punishment should not be so severe that it permanently damages the parent-child relationship.* Naturally some short-term unpleasantness will temporarily alter the relationship; punishment is not meant to be enjoyable. If it is, the child or parent has some mixed-up emotions, or the punishment wasn't really a punishment at all. But punishment should not poison the air between parent and child in any long-term way. You must have a way to restore the good feelings between you. How this happens varies from family to family, but the need is universal. If a cloud hangs between the two of you and just gradually goes away as time passes, only to reappear the next time you must punish, you need to take a look at the punishment process again. A caution: the "making up" can sometimes be so pleasant that, as young couples say, "It's worth the fight." Don't fall into that trap. The aim is to restore your normal relationship, not to provide an emotional lollipop.

5. *Punishment should not damage the child.* Of course a parent should take care not to physically hurt a child. (I will make some comments on unsuitable physical punishments in the section on spanking.) But he should also make sure he doesn't verbally abuse the child; ridicule, sarcasm, and belittlement wear down a child's spirit. Remember, too, that harsh, excessive punishment may distort the child's view of adults and make it difficult for him to relate emotionally to other people. A child's view of the Heavenly Father may be similarly twisted by the impressions he gets of earthly fathers. The basic preventive guideline is this: good punishment does not maim or deform the child either physically, emotionally, mentally, or spiritually.

6. *Punishment should be appropriate to the individual child.* The key question is, Can the child learn from it? An especially important consideration is the child's age. For example, if you decide to punish a child by isolating him in his room, the time

limit of the isolation ought to be different for a four-year-old than for a fourteen-year-old. When a parent doesn't understand how a child's age affects his learning capacity, he may abuse the child unknowingly. He may, for example, punish a two-year-old by placing the child on a chair for fifteen minutes. The child, having very limited comprehension of time, almost immediately scrambles down and resumes the misbehavior. Now his parent slams him roughly into the chair, saying, "I told you to stay there!" If the child were seven, a fifteen-minute time-out might be suitable, especially if the child could watch a clock to time his own punishment. But in this instance the sophistication of the punishment isn't matched to the child's maturity. The punishment must also be appropriate for the child's personality. One child is genuinely affected by a mild reproof, which brings about the desired change in behavior. Another child may respond better if you give him an extra chore to do.

7. *Punishment should fit the deed.* All of us understand the injustice in the classic story of Jean Paul Jean, who was imprisoned for stealing a loaf of bread to feed his starving children. Even if important principles lie behind relatively minor misdeeds, we still cannot expect our children to accept and profit from punishments which are disproportionate to the seriousness of the misdeed.

Many parents have found it helpful to rethink their use of punishment, especially if they find they are punishing quite often. All of our children are doing some things we want them to do. Ask yourself the question, "How do I get him to do the things he is doing right?" Then try to figure out how you can effectively use these methods in the situations in which you usually have to resort to punishment.

Child rearing is hard work and takes intelligence and imagination, especially if you bring a new child into your family. You may not be able to rely on the methods that are effective with your other children because this child is used to different rules and different treatment.

Rewarding, ignoring, and punishing all have their place in discipline; you should use them in thoughtful, well-intentioned ways. But what about spanking? Some years ago I came to the conclusion that there are good reasons to avoid using physical punishment, particularly when raising children not biologically your own. Among those reasons are the following ones.

Most important to remember is that many children come to us from homes in which they were abused. They don't understand or profit from mild physical punishment because they have been conditioned to respond to harsh physical punishment, administered often. Certainly we don't want to use punishment of this kind or frequency. But just the basic facts about physical punishment should make us seriously question our use of it.

First of all, we must keep in mind that a parent tends to increase the amount of physical punishment he uses, especially if it isn't working well or if it is working too well. That is, if a mild spanking doesn't work, a parent tends to try a harder one. Or if that hard spanking did work, he may try it again when something less severe would have worked just as well, simply because the spanking method is "tried and true."

In addition, we must remember that physical punishment—more than other kinds of punishment, perhaps—may feed our aggressive instincts. Some experimental evidence suggests that when we hit we don't "get it out of our system" but only become angrier. In other words, our violent feelings are not in a cistern which we empty when we express our violence; they may be contained in a well which keeps refilling as we draw from it.

I have known a good many abusive parents, and they are not different than I am by nature. We are different only in the way we express ourselves to our children. Realizing what a fine line separates us, I must avoid those kinds of punishment—perhaps physical punishment—that might encourage me to be abusive.

If you decide that physical punishment is appropriate in your family, I urge you to set some very definite and limited guidelines for it. Remember that all of the cautions and guidelines for punishment in general apply to physical punishment.

In addition, the following cautions apply specifically to physical punishment: never shake a child (he may suffer significant brain damage); never box ears (eardrums may be broken); never twist arms or legs (bones may be broken); never use poisonous substances such as detergents in the mouth (the child may swallow them or suck them into his lungs). Well-meaning parents have harmed their children in all of these ways in a moment of exasperation or frustration.

What the Bible Says about Punishment

A fund of child-rearing advice is summed up in the expression "Spare the rod and spoil the child." Unfortunately, carelessly used Scripture is sometimes quoted to justify what amounts to child abuse. For this and other reasons I want to discuss both the use and misuse of the Jewish and Christian teachings on child rearing.

The principle that children need discipline and guidance to grow up well is part of our religious heritage. But when we try to discover what the Bible says about rearing children (and specifically about the use of physical punishment), we need to consider everything the Bible says about the children of the covenant family, both in the old and new testaments. *All* that the Bible has to say about nurturing and training children is important, not just the most widely known or quoted verses.

True, certain verses do seem to aptly summarize biblical teaching. For example, Ephesians 6:4 summarizes the general scriptural message that parents should raise their children to know God: "Fathers, provoke not your children to wrath: but bring them up in the nurture and admonition of the Lord." I have also found it helpful to examine my child rearing by turning around the idea found in Hebrews 12: "As a father who loves his son disciplines him, so the Lord disciplines you." As I consider how the Heavenly Father deals with me, I gain understanding about how I am to deal with my children.

But we must be careful not to quote particular verses as the proof-text answer to almost any situation. One verse that we tend to use too often is Proverbs 22:15: "Foolishness is bound in the heart of a child; but the rod of correction shall drive it far from him." A verse similarly used is Proverbs 13:24: "He that spareth his rod hateth his son: but he that loveth him chasteneth him betimes." And sometimes a parent gives an order and then throws the full weight of God's authority behind his order by quoting Ephesians 6:1: "Children, obey your parents in the Lord, for this is right." To avoid well-intentioned but indiscriminate use of these passages, I try to follow three principles when I consider what a specific verse has to say about discipline.

1. *The entire Bible is the context for any particular verse.* Let's use as a specific example Proverbs 22:15, one of the verses quoted above : "Foolishness is bound in the heart of a child...." We know that the Bible teaches that it is the Holy Spirit's work to convict us of our sin and to apply Christ's redeeming power to our hearts to renew us; we cannot drive sin away by physical punishment. Thus this verse certainly cannot mean that we can "beat the devil" out of a child—which it is sometimes misinterpreted to suggest. Rather, it suggests that children, like all of us, are inclined to sin, and that all of us need to be corrected because of this tendency. Such an interpretation is consistent with Old Testament texts like Isaiah 53:6 or New Testament texts like Romans 6:23-24.

2. *We must determine whether the language being used is literal, poetic, or symbolic;* we must also decide on the best English translation of the original words. A good verse to analyze is Job 36:10: "He openeth also their ear to discipline." The word for discipline—*musar*—is sometimes translated "chastisement," sometimes as "instruction." Obviously, the sense here is not literal—God does not box our ears—so "instruction" is probably intended.

We must use similar interpretive logic when we use the verse from Proverbs quoted earlier—"He that spareth his rod hateth his son, but he that loveth him chasteneth him betimes." The word for chasten is *musar*; the word for rod is *shebet,* which can mean a long rod of *any* kind—a shepherd's staff, a sword, a scepter. Certainly the rendering of the King James Version just quoted is very valuable and accurate, a rendering of the Scriptures that has influenced all later translations. But we must remember that it was made in an age much more physically violent than ours; thus the choice of words was probably influenced by the culture of the time. We must also remember that *shebet* is used in different ways in different passages of the Bible: it is a rod of comfort in both

Psalm 23 and Micah 7:14, where the prophet prays, "Feed thy people with Thy rod."

Keeping such things in mind, we should realize that this verse can be translated as "He that spareth his *scepter* [symbol of authority] hateth his son, but he that loveth him *instructs* him betimes." This interpretation is consistent with the New Testament emphasis on discipline, which shows that God sometimes uses difficult experiences to chasten us.

3. *We must strive to be aware of the social context* of a practice and look beyond particular behaviors to principles. For example, in Mosaic Law (Deut. 21:13-21), parents were instructed to bring their rebellious son to the elders, make their complaint, and deliver him up for public stoning.

To properly understand this instruction we must consider the historical setting. A nomadic people without boy's schools or jails was confronted with a young adult who would not carry his share of the load and was wasting the family's resources. His refusal to help could well endanger the survival of his whole family, because everyone was needed to earn a living from the land. In fact, in cultures round about, parents had life-and-death control over children, but Israel was instructed to carry out a public civil procedure; then the proper authorities would pronounce judgment. The principle appears to be that the family was to take responsibility for its deviant members, and to seek the help of the appropriate authorities when they had exhausted their resources. But there is no scriptural record that this drastic punishment was actually carried out, though it may have been. And certainly, because of our different social circumstances today, we should not follow the letter of this law.

The Hebrew psalm reads, "Children are a gift from the Lord." We do not own them, but we are privileged to help them grow up. It is our responsibility to guard them from harm, to provide them with good as we are able, and to permit them to mature with our guidance and help. Our authority over them is limited by the commandments of the God who gives them to us to nurture.

I will close this section with a rather lengthy story because it illustrates a number of ideas about the Bible and discipline, and punishment as part of discipline. It shows the limited nature of our parental wisdom, and the consequent need for humility and grace in our discipline. It also shows how all of the Scriptures—not just an isolated verse—become the context for discipline, and how faithfully God helps us as we struggle to discipline our children in a way that pleases Him.

One day as I was emptying wastebaskets, I came across a game that only a few days before had been lying safely on a shelf. The game had been deliberately broken apart in order to remove a quantity of BB shot, and the BB shot was gone. I reacted strongly to what I saw. As I mentioned in the section on "snowballing," major values may be reflected in our reaction to fairly minor incidents. In this case I was disturbed at the deliberate destruction of the usefulness of the game (we teach the concept of stewardship of possessions), and I was concerned that the BB shot might find its way into some dangerous pastime.

When I confronted my child with the broken game, he admitted breaking it to get the BB's. I scolded him quite severely, and then demanded the BB's. When the child told me he could not remember what he did with them, I did not believe him and told him so. I confined him to his room as punishment, and told him he must stay there until he gave me the BB's or accounted for them. He came out of his room only for supper; at bedtime the incident was still unresolved. Two days went by, and still he had nothing, spending all of his free time alone in his room. His father came home from a trip, heard the story, talked and prayed with him, and was unable to learn any more than I had. All the family knew about the problem and was praying for a satisfactory outcome. A week of talking, praying, and confinement passed. By then my dilemma was apparent. His punishment had now exceeded what was appropriate for the original offense, but I kept thinking to myself, "I can't forgive him and be reconciled until he confesses."

As I thought about my problem, various scripture passages came to mind, and one passage in particular haunted me: "But God commendeth his love toward us, in that while we were yet sinners, Christ died for us." God loves and accepts us because Christ died for us, not because we do something, not because we confess our sin. We are unable to forgive and accept one another on the same basis—the finished work of Christ—not because our brother or sister or child fulfills our requirements for reconciliation with us. When I realized that this principle also applied to my relationship with my child, I knew that I could forgive him.

Using language suited to his age, I explained to my child what I had been thinking, and offered him forgiveness. I told him I would not bring up the BB's again, but he could if he wished; then I prayed with him, hugged him, and sent him out to play. I told the rest of the family what we had done.

Several weeks later I was working in the kitchen. The child had borrowed my stepstool and was busy in his room dusting and rearranging his bookshelves. Suddenly he was beside me shouting, "I found them! I found them!" In his hand was a small amber mug, half-full of BB shot. His joy made it obvious to me that this was a true discovery. He now remembered putting them there for safekeeping. Did my angry scolding drive the memory from him? Did God withhold the memory so both of us could learn a lesson about forgiveness? We showed the BB's to the family at supper, and thanked God in family worship for finding the BB's. Later I poured them into a small plastic bag and put them away. They became for me another Ebenezer stone, a reminder that "hitherto hath the Lord helped us."

How to Handle Special Discipline Problems

He won't accept my authority. Probably every American child has said to someone trying to control his behavior, "I don't have to listen to you. You're not my mother." He is recognizing two things. One, that his mother or father has a right to tell him things to which he should listen. Two, that in our society at least, others don't have that same power over him. He may not do so directly, but very often the child joining the restructured family is saying, "I don't have to listen to you because you are not my parent." This problem may be obviously or subtly complicating discipline in your home. How will you handle it?

Politically we have determined that governments should operate with "the consent of the governed." In the restructured family, you may need to try winning the child's consent to be governed. I think it is useless to try to resort to a straight power play; remember that even the most rigid dictatorships eventually seem to fail. You can force obedience to a certain extent, but ultimately you will lose the battle for allegiance. Some children, especially younger ones, may readily agree that you should govern them because you have the job of parent in the home. But how can you win consent from a more reluctant child so that you may begin to function as a family whose parents are primarily responsible for setting and enforcing standards?

When I asked that question of a woman who has helped many functional families, she said, "The child will learn to accept your authority and standards as his relationship with you grows. As he learns you care about him, he will care about you and want to copy you." Her answer has helped me.

If a child is to accept your authority, you must show him that you genuinely care about him as an individual. Of course you care about your reputation and about what other people think of your family. But the child must be able to believe that most of all you care about him. If a child senses that the rules are primarily meant to make you look good rather than to help him, he may deliberately disobey or reject them.

You must also live by the standards you establish for the child. If I expect my child to tell the truth, I cannot ask my husband to say "she isn't here" when my long-winded neighbor calls. If the child is not to shoplift, I must not bring home postage stamps or ball-point pens from the office. You need to be very careful to demonstrate the honesty, compassion, and self-control that you ask of the child. He will notice your hypocrisies.

In addition, allow him to participate, so far as he is able, in setting the standards that govern him. That is one way children express their wish to be part of the family. Help him understand how the standards developed and what they are supposed to accomplish. Explain any traditional family rule that is foreign to him.

All of this will not happen overnight: the process of winning consent may take time and involve many difficult experiences. Neither is winning consent a once-and-for-all proposition. We are used to the idea that an official may win an election and interpret that as our consent to be governed by him. But the degree to which we consent may rise and fall during his term in office, and we may even vote against him in the next election—unless he perpetually works at winning and keeping our consent. Similarly, the functional parent must not take his position for granted. He must continually try to strengthen the parent-child relationship on which his authority partially rests.

I'm starting "in the hole." When a child joins your family, you frequently develop this feeling for various reasons. Perhaps you are in the habit of using minimal punishment, but the child who comes to live with you has been spanked hard and often. He doesn't think a parent is really serious until the parent reaches for a paddle. Another child has gotten so used to being nagged six or seven times before he obeys that he never listens to you until you get very upset and start yelling. The reverse can be true, too. Your new child may be used to minimal correction, but you are used to yelling at your other thick-skinned children. Even though there is love and warmth beneath what you say, the child is wounded by your ranting. Or your new child may be a handful. You are used to kids who misbehave and have to be corrected once in a while, but this one seems to be in trouble all of the time. No sooner do you settle one problem than he creates another. You don't know where to begin.

The first situation (overuse of physical punishment) calls for much adaptation on your part, especially at first. You can modify the way you treat the child so that your disciplinary style isn't completely foreign to him. But you may need to change his expectations, too—especially if what he is used to is basically destructive. My husband and I felt neck-deep in trouble when a four-year-old boy joined our family several years ago. Rex had come from a home in which he had been routinely abused physically. He was hostile, sullen, and aggressive much of the time; he was also bright and mischievous. Naturally he got into quite a bit of trouble. Unfortunately, it was hard to convince him that any punishment short of being whipped with a belt was serious. Still worse, he did not know how to get the attention and love he craved by behaving, but he knew a hundred and one ways to get our attention by making us angry.

We had to change this destructive behavior because it not only hurt Rex but it hurt his relationship with us. I discovered that he brought out the worst in me and my family. We had to struggle constantly to keep from reacting as Rex seemed to want us to react, and to look for positive ways to give him attention. We had to take the initiative to hug and hold him; he didn't come seeking our love. We had to find ways to manage and change his bad behavior that didn't just perpetuate his seeking abuse. Starting "in the hole" like this is fairly common; it is one of the challenges of raising a child that joins your family.

Perhaps it will help if I illustrate how we attempted to change a pattern of behavior that was bad for Rex, and that made us react negatively toward him. His table manners made mealtimes unbearable for all of us—he grabbed any food he could reach, ate with his hands, spilled much food without meaning to, and threw additional quantities of it if he became upset. Our plan to deal with this was worked out as a family one evening after Rex was asleep, with everyone contributing ideas and assuming responsibilities. As you will note, our plans illustrate earlier suggestions in the chapter about restructuring, individualizing, discussing, and so forth.

We decided to move all family meals from the dining room to the basement, where we had indoor-outdoor carpeting and a kitchen table and chairs. This would simplify cleanup and lower concern about ruining family possessions. We rearranged seating so that each of the older two girls had a pre-schooler to supervise, the third girl could conveniently serve the table as necessary, and Dad could assume my "hostessing" duties. This left me free to concentrate on Rex, who was seated at the end of the table in a youth chair that had arms that permitted us to pull him close to the table, and thus minimized his ability to reach food for himself or scramble down from his seat. I set his place with only the bare minimum of utensils—a plate and spoon—so that he would learn to use them. Several times during the course of the meal I handed him a glass that had only a small amount of milk or juice in it, and I placed only small quantities of food on his plate at a time. I respected his choice of foods to eat and removed promptly any food he indicated he was not going to eat. If he threw the food, he was promptly removed from the table, and the meal ended for him and for me. All this was done to set up a situation in which we could offer many more words of praise and encouragement than words of reproof. While we were working to improve his skill in eating, we did not worry about balanced meals or other related issues. We had decided our priority was improvement in his relationship with the family at mealtimes.

Perhaps you wonder where Rex went when he left the table. When Rex first came to live with us, we needed to find a way to confine him—when he was in one of his more violent moods—without inflicting harm or letting him harm himself. This too required a well-thought-out and persistently applied strategy. We chose to put him in a playpen in the middle of the living room. A folding screen became a visual barrier between us, but I could still sense when he got out of the playpen and could immediately put him back. We found it also helped Rex if we set up a sound barrier—lively, loud music on the stereo. He howled and cursed and kicked at first, but eventually he learned to use the playpen as a place to settle down and get control of himself. At first, when even for a few seconds he stopped attempting to get out and became quiet, we gave him an M & M and verbal rewards and hugs. But being confined became distasteful enough to him that he learned to control his behavior without the incentive of the playpen. When Rex accomplished this, we were able to go on to help him change other behaviors.

The more distorted the child's patterns of behavior, the more urgent it is that the whole family become involved in such changes. You will need to do much thinking and planning. Set priorities, don't attempt too much at a time, be prepared for setbacks, and use trial and error freely to find a way to meet the challenges such a child presents. And base your plan on strongly encouraging good behavior, not simply on punishment of the behavior you want to get rid of. Always remember that such a troubled child needs your help—even if he doesn't appear to want it.

Similarly challenging is the child who seems to constantly misbehave. You feel the ratio of bad to good behavior is just hopeless. If the child has just come to live with you, it may help you to know about the "honeymoon" effect. Quite often when a child first joins a family, he behaves extremely well. His new parents may be surprised and happy that this child (who may have been troublesome in the past) is behaving beautifully. Then the roof falls in. In a few days—or perhaps even a few months—after he arrives, he is suddenly up to all of his old tricks, plus a few new ones. This radical change in behavior is not uncommon; you should handle it as calmly and firmly as possible. The child has simply become secure enough to begin testing your limits. When he finds that you do stand firm, he will work his way back to better behavior. Perhaps it won't quite be "honeymoon" quality, but it will improve.

A child who has been frequently moved from home to home may behave badly to see if you will move him again. In a way, the child is trying to take charge of his own life. He seems to be saying, "I'll force them to move me in response to what I do, not because of someone or something I can't control." He may sorely test your patience before you convince him by words and actions that you intend to keep him. If the child has always been considered hard to handle and you have never seen him behave well, you may want to get some outside help to improve his behavior before it permanently damages your relationship. A planned intervention program like behavior modification may help you both.

This really bugs me. Sometimes as you look at general family discipline or at your discipline of a particular child, you can objectively say that things are going well. Yet there is a particular behavior that really bothers you, and you tend to over-react to it or find that it gets in the way of handling un-related problems. Let me give you an example.

When Shirley was ten years old she was a very finicky eater. She was a small child with a very small appetite. Per-haps that was partly the reason that she often came to the table and announced that she didn't like a thing being served.

She complained frequently and persistently about the food. Talking to her about it, asking her to leave the table if she didn't like the food, attempting to serve her favorite more frequently—none of these strategies worked. Her younger brother began to copy her behavior, often when I knew he did like the food. I was really annoyed.

After discussing the situation together, my husband and I decided to try behavior modification to see if we could put an end to the complaining. The steps for a behavior modification program are these: (1) Get a clear picture of the behavior you wish to eliminate—when it happens, how often, where, etc. (2) Set a clear goal for new behavior. (3) Spell out the reward for the desired behavior and the terms of getting the reward. (4) Ignore all of the behavior you are trying to eliminate and reward the desired behavior. (5) Continue rewarding desired behavior at decreasing intervals until the new behavior is well established.

Sound complicated? This is the way my husband and I set up our program, step by step: (1) We agreed that the behavior we wanted to stop was Shirley's complaining about the food at the supper table. (2) We discussed the situation with Shirley and together set this goal: that she would stop complaining about the food. We worked out the rest of the program with her, too, since we believe that the child should be included as much as possible in attempts to change his behavior. A child is a responsible human being. (3) We agreed that Shirley would come to the table and make no negative comments about the food. So long as she chose one serving of food from each of the four basic food groups (which she knew from studying nutrition in school), I would not ask her to eat any particular food. If she did this, at bedtime I would bring her a snack I knew she liked. (4) We stopped responding in any way to any negative comments Shirley made about the food, but we accepted any compliments from her very warmly—and rewarded her with snacks. (5) After two weeks Shirley had stopped complaining, and we gave her bedtime treats only occasionally. We continued to be appreciative of her new table manners. And it really did work! In fact, when she was thirteen, I had a new problem: how to find *enough* food to fill up that always-empty girl. (I should warn you that her older sisters were not sure it was fair to reward Shirley for something that they were already doing "for nothing." You have to handle this problem separately.)

It sometimes seems to us parents that children use an unfair form of behavior modification on us. Instead of plainly asking for the things they want, they try to manipulate us into giving them what they want. A mother complained to me once that her adopted son would never ask for second helpings at the table (first helpings were passed around to all) but would try all sorts of tricks to get food sent his way without asking. She felt ashamed of her irritation at this behavior, but she resented it nonetheless because she felt it reflected his unwillingness to accept her and her husband as giving parents. No doubt she was partly right in her guess, but her son may also have had trouble believing that she wanted to give him good things and that he deserved them. He was avoiding open rejection by avoiding direct requests. To handle this problem, talk about such feelings with your child, and make it clear that you love him and want him to ask you for things.

How can I prevent snowballing? Snowballing occurs when a relatively minor misdeed gets mixed up with important values and feelings and develops into a major issue. Let me illustrate what I mean. A couple has three children of middle-school age, and ordinarily the mother gets up in the morning to fix breakfast and send the kids off to school and her husband to work. But she has been extremely busy lately and is also fighting off a head cold, so one weeknight she cuts grapefruit for breakfast, puts out clean socks for everybody, and provides for any minor crisis she can think of. Before going to bed she announces that she would like to sleep in the next morning and that every child will get a treat for breakfast—a jelly donut. But in the morning she is awakened by yelling and crying. When it doesn't die down in a couple of minutes, she gets out of bed, grabs a robe—no time for slippers—and goes downstairs to see who is killing whom. Youngest son complains bitterly that someone ate his donut while he was feeding the dog. Both older brothers noisily insist that they never touched his donut. Eldest brother adds that youngest probably ate the donut himself and now is trying to get them into trouble. Unlikely, Mother thinks, but of course it is possible.

The noise gets worse as she tries to sift through all of the charges and countercharges. Half-shaved, her husband stalks angrily into the kitchen. Now the threats and accusations really start to fly. Dad: "None of you will go anywhere for a month if it takes that long to get to the bottom of this!" Mother: "None of you cares if I get sick and die of pneumonia!" Oldest son: "You can lock me up for a year. Who cares!" Youngest son: "I hate this whole family!" What a mess. Finally Dad realizes that he is going to be late for work and storms out of the house; the kids leave for school—one tearful, one angry, one sullen; and Mother sits down to take stock of a miserable situation. The crime has now changed from donut-snitching on impulse to premeditated lying and stealing plus "mother abuse." The punishment proposed is house imprisonment for an indeterminate period. This is snowballing! What can you do to prevent it?

The first step is to try to think through the situation and determine why everyone got so upset about a relatively minor incident. There can be all kinds of contributing reasons, but in the illustration just given there are probably just two or three principal causes. For one thing, major values became an issue in the situation, since this family puts a high premium on honesty. One child's minor theft and subsequent lie hurt and shocked both parents. In addition, the mother is upset that her children were so inconsiderate to her after she had gone out of her way for them. The donuts were meant to be for them what the opportunity to sleep was for her: a special treat. She also may be quite concerned that the children aren't learning to get along better, especially if hers is a newly formed functional family.

Next the parents must make a plan to unroll the snowball, to scale the situation back down to its proper proportions. In this case it would probably help to spell out to the children the underlying reasons for the big uproar. Then the parents might let the children settle the donut business among themselves.

You may be thinking, "But those values are important to me, too, and I think that solution would let the children off too easily." But the parents have already made clear to their children how important honesty is to them; they probably don't need to emphasize their point further. The children now need an opportunity to demonstrate to their parents and themselves that they do care about Mother, about each other, and about honesty. If a similar incident were repeated within days, the parents might then conclude that something more serious was involved than impulsive donut-snitching and an equally impulsive lie. But that's a major problem, not the snowballing of a minor problem, which is what we started out to discuss in this illustration.

When shall I put my foot down? Many parents who accept an older child into their family don't know when to start being firm. They don't think they can expect the child to listen to them and behave well at first, yet they realize that at some point they will have to insist that he does.

Earlier I indicated that it is a good idea to clear up many problems and set important limits before the child joins the family. Trouble often starts when there are no apparent preliminary problems, but the child becomes a terror when he moves in. If you let him "get away with murder" at first, you will probably make discipline much more difficult for both of you in the long run. It is worth knowing that parents who have added older children to their families usually say that they should have been firmer sooner than they were! However, it may be that this is twenty-twenty hindsight, and that their common-sense ideas and intuition about what the child could accept guided them to hold off as long as they did. Perhaps they could not have enforced stricter limits sooner. If a rule is important to you, enforce it as soon as you can so that you don't become resentful or frustrated about it. But don't get caught up in a rush of minor regulations.

Part of the difficulty in setting limits may stem from your own ambivalence about whether you have the same right to set the parental standards for this child. This is a problem you'll need to solve for yourself. But remember that you are raising this child as a parent would—therefore you do have the right to exert parental control. Perhaps the source of the trouble is the fact that one parent is a step-parent, and thus the child thinks he has less right to set limits. Face this problem openly—first with the step-parent, then with the child.

If you treat a child more leniently at first than you do later, make sure you consciously decide to do so. Don't base your decision on any imagined lack of authority. Base it instead of your desire to help the child adapt to your home without overwhelming him.

CHAPTER **4**

MAINTAINING RELATION-SHIPS WITH THE BIOLOGICAL FAMILY

Why Bother?

In the introduction I described some of the people for whom this book was written, and I described the book's subject: all of those children who have one or two living biological parents, but who make their home with another family. But the situation is often more complex than that. Besides his functional family, a child often has a large family of relatives—not only parents but uncles, cousins, grandparents, and so forth. One of the child's tasks is coming to terms with his relationship to that biological family, something his functional family can and should help him do.

Sometimes a parent will say to me, "I don't think Susie has any memory of living with her own family. She never says a word about it." Or a step-parent will say, "I have no idea how John feels about trying to see his Dad sometimes. He refuses to talk about it even if I bring the subject up." Other children have lost their families long ago and seem so completely comfortable in their new homes that it seems almost unnecessary and unfair to remind them of their "differentness" by mentioning a biological family. In these and a hundred similar situations, a functional parent is wondering, "Is it really that important to bother with the relationship to the biological family?" My answer, and that of many others who work with children, is an emphatic "Yes!" Let me explain why.

1. *A child's seeming indifference to the subject or apparent lack of memory may mask deep-seated hurt that has not healed.* We say that time heals all wounds, but this adage isn't always true. You can help a child cope with these feelings only if both of

you accept and explore his relationship to his biological family.

2. *The child knows he has biological parents somewhere;* no child believes that he was found under a large cabbage leaf. He has probably developed his own explanation about why he does not live with those parents—an explanation very likely based on false bits of information, stories he has read, and pure imagination. Unfortunately, he almost certainly assumes that he is to blame for the fact that he does not live with his biological parent or parents. Deep inside he believes that this means he is less worthy and lovable than children who do live with their parents. Even if this is a subconscious belief, it nevertheless influences his self-image negatively.

3. *He has probably created a set of fantasy parents who embody all that he wishes his parents could be.* I suspect that many children create such fantasy parents, and that such imaginings account for the widespread appeal of fairy tales about lost princes and princesses. I remember the elaborate fantasies that my sister and I spent hours constructing. In these tales we had the best of everything: expensive clothes, elaborate homes, beautiful parents, fantastic parties—and no brothers! Of course, the child living with his biological parents must sooner or later confront reality. His nose looks very much like his dad's; her mother's oddly shaped brown eyes are very much like her own. For better or for worse these are his parents, and he must learn to accept them and his resemblance to them.

But maintaining fantasies is much easier for the child living with another family, or living with only one biological parent. Especially if he never sees or hears of his biological family, the fantasy family merges with the biological family to become his "real" family. Then he can secretly think, "If I lived with my 'real' family they would understand me. They would let me do this. They wouldn't be cross and upset. My stepmother is a witch. My 'real' mother would love me instead of hollering at me." Instead of struggling with the difficult problem of identifying with yet separating himself from his parents, as every child must do, he can too easily escape into a world of make-believe where all is well. This is why it is so important that he gets to know his biological family, that he sees them as real people with weaknesses as well as strengths. Of course he will use his functional parents as models, too, especially if his relationship with them is strong and warm.

4. *The uninformed child will grow into the man or woman who needs concrete information about his biological background.* During a medical crisis, when he marries, at the birth of his first child—these are times when he might have a strong desire or an actual need for specific information. Gathering the facts at such a late date may be more difficult, more painful, and less clearly meaningful than early discovery would be. It is best if the child has available to him as early as possible all relevant information about his genetic heritage, the health of his parents and other close relatives, causes of deaths, etc. If you wonder what information your child will probably need, get a copy of a good medical/social history form from a medical clinic or a social agency and complete it as best you can. Then pass the information on to the child as it seems appropriate, and let him know that you keep records for him in the same place other valuable family papers are kept. *Important:* Do not include gossip or hurtful judgmental statements in this record.

5. *The culture in which this child is growing up considers bloodlines important, whether you do or not.* As both a foster parent and an adoptive parent I sympathize deeply with those who feel that we make too much of blood ties and too little of love ties in our legal and social communities. But I know I cannot change all at once the world in which my children are growing up, and neither can you. Our culture has a hundred ways of saying that bloodlines are important: "Blood will tell." "Blood is thicker than water." "Who is your *real* mother?" In fact, each one of my older children has been asked to write a report for school in which he or she traced the family tree. Such situations put tremendous pressure on the child.

Recognizing that blood ties are significant in our culture, my husband and I have tried to teach our adopted children something about *both* of their families, and give them pride in both. We are glad that our adopted sons usually answer casual questions about their family by referring to us, but we also understand if sometimes they choose to use information about their biological family. If a child has not completely severed legal ties with his biological family, he may be even more inclined to identify with them in certain situations. I think he should be free to do this, provided his information is accurate.

6. *There may be legal reasons why the child should maintain a relationship with his biological family.* Among these are the following: he may be entitled to social security benefits; he may qualify for certain funds if his father is a veteran; he may be entitled to property or insurance benefits. Occasionally such benefits are not claimed simply because no one close to the child is aware that they are due him.

I list these reasons for maintaining contact with the biological family because I know how reluctant we can sometimes be to do it. We have come to love so dearly the children we are raising that we have a tendency to think of them as part of our family only. Sometimes we resist contact with a biological family because we know that something about the relationship hurts the child. The story of Laura illustrates how real that danger is, and yet how necessary it still may be to maintain the contact. As an infant Laura was the victim of parental abuse; she grew up horribly crippled, disfigured, and mute in a foundling home run by Catholic nuns. Her story is told in *No Language But A Cry* by Dr. Richard D'Ambrosio, the psychiatrist who helped bring her back to emotional life.

Laura began to talk only after more than two years of regular work with Dr. D'Ambrosio. He used a playhouse and a family of dolls, patiently creating various scenes to try to penetrate her fantasy world. Finally she broke the wall of silence with "No, no, no!" when he recreated a scene in which a tiny baby doll was abused by her parents. After Laura was talking freely with Dr. D'Ambrosio, she told him about the fantasy mother she had created for herself. This mother was beautiful, loving, and generous. Often she brought Laura presents, especially the shiny new shoes that Laura loved. Her fantasy father was handsome and kind and good. The dark part of this fantasy was Laura's belief that she could not live with them because she was so ugly.

When Laura was well along in her recovery, her biological father reappeared for one visit. He promised to telephone nightly and to come again in a week. As you might expect, Laura's father and this person become one in her mind. When her real father never telephoned or came again, Laura was desolate. She lashed out at herself and at all of the people at the institution. Although it took weeks for her to recover and begin to make progress again, she was ultimately wiser and more accepting of herself. She was able to forsake the fantasy father and forgive the genuine one.

Just before Laura was to begin her first job outside the orphanage, her biological mother reappeared, and she too wanted to visit. Laura agreed to see her with a beloved nun present, and she was respectful and reserved. Her mother, puzzled by this self-possessed young woman who resisted her blandishments, finally dumped out as a gift to her a brown bag of shoes. Laura reacted with terrible emotion, screaming, "No, you're not my mother! Go away!" The astonished nun sent the mother out and quieted Laura. But knowing Laura's fantasy makes her reaction understandable. The contrast between the shoes of her fantasy and the scuffed and dirty shoes her mother brought her made Laura realize that this mother had nothing to give her. Fortunately she did not regress as she had after her father's visit, and she soon was able to evaluate her mother as a real person. Because Laura had received love and support from parental substitutes, she could give up her fantasy parents, see reality with its pain, and develop a mature acceptance of her biological parents.

Laura's story is extreme; most absent parents have more to offer their children. Yet even in this case the child needed to come to terms with the reality of her parents' humanness before she could accept herself as a worthy person. As Laura's case proves, trying to "blot out" the biological family can be dangerous: the unexpected intrusion of a long-absent parent, for example, can upset the best-intentioned silence. If you take the initiative in the relationship with the other family, you are more likely to be able to control the timing of meetings with family members, and to help the child deal with them constructively. If contact with the biological parents is not possible, the child needs other means to help him outgrow his fantasy, especially if his fantasy makes him think negatively about himself.

If you are discussing a child's parents with him, try to avoid some of the more common mistakes. The child can usually assess adult behavior quite well; it only confuses him and makes him wary if you invent things about the absent parents' character or behavior. You should also avoid constantly criticizing the absent parents. This may make the child feel defensive and resentful. It will also make him wonder about himself. If his parents are "bad," is he "bad"? To avoid these problems, constantly examine your motives. Are you really helping the child face reality? Or are you trying to win his affection by blackballing his biological parents? Take care not to be insensitive in the name of doing good.

How to Make Visits Constructive

I have discussed the reasons for maintaining contact with the child's biological parents. Now I'll suggest how a child's visits with them can best be handled.

The child has to decide for himself how he will relate to the important people in his life. Those who work with children believe the child does this best when he is permitted ongoing contact with these people in positive circumstances. If he is supported and encouraged, he can handle much confusion, sort out many conflicts, and develop relationships with varying degrees of intimacy. The child permitted to control his own emotional life develops good coping skills. If parents deny him this control he may have a great deal of catching up to do later, when the conflicts he faces may be much more difficult to work out. In addition, parents who alienate a child from his cultural, biological, and spiritual roots often discover that as a young adult he longs for them, for the opportunity to understand and appreciate them.

Visiting is part of your attempt to let the child develop an identity that is partly bound up with you, because you are important to him—but also partly bound up with his biological parent or family. Helping the child with visiting is part of your special responsibility. By "visiting" I mean every possible kind of contact between the child and his biological family, from his discussing them with you and receiving occasional postcards from them, to his calling and visiting them frequently.

Establish guidelines for visiting. The kind of unplanned, disruptive contact that gets called "visiting" is a sore subject with many families who are absorbed in the difficulties and challenges of raising children. A child's new family can easily resent the added burden that visiting places on them. But the following basic guidelines can help make visiting less of an anathema.

1. *Make visiting part of a larger goal of developing and maintaining responsible relationships.* Most of us have a tendency to think of visiting as a right to be denied or permitted. For instance, you may have thought, "A parent like that has no right to see his son." Or you may have argued in more formal "caseworker" langauge, "No one has a right to a destructive relationship." And you may have heard some challenges like this: "Don't I have a right to see my own grandchild?"

Putting the question of visiting into a context of "rights" is almost certain to produce situations in which various rights will clash—the biological parent's right, the child's right, your right, and so on. You may bitterly disagree about whose rights should prevail, or about who should judge the hierarchy of rights. The last resort may be to determine legal rights. But the law is very poorly equipped to deal with relationships between people. The court can order, but human beings implement the orders, and all of us know that complying with the letter of the law can be technically just and at the same time sabotage the law's intent. In addition, moral rights and legal rights might get confused. What the court cannot order in the name of either law or equity, impartial and reasonable people might agree should be determined on a moral basis. But who will determine these moral rights?

Others think of visits as rewards and denial of visits as punishments. You may have caught yourself saying to your child, "If you don't behave yourself, I won't let you call your sister." You might also have told a parent that he can't see his child unless he makes his support payments promptly.

A visiting framework which emphasizes responsible relationships creates a positive context in which to determine a course of action. Each person is asked to be responsible for the effect of his own actions on himself and on all other persons affected by them. Rather than staging the confrontation that seems to characterize any discussion of rights, or employing the manipulation of rewards and punishments, reasonable people can in this way arrive at reasonable solutions to visiting problems. Of course, none of us behaves reasonably or responsibly all of the time, but it is a goal worth pursuing.

2. *Make sure visits have explicit goals, whether they are spelled out or not.* In addition, each participant should think about and help determine the goals for visiting. And all participants need to recognize hidden goals as well as acknowledged goals. For example, in a fairly simple case in which a ten-year-old boy is living with his mother and visiting his remarried father, the acknowledged goals might include the following:

Child: To stay acquainted with my Dad.

Mother: To provide my son with opportunities to identify with his Dad. To get some help in carrying out the goals we both have for our son.

Father: To fulfill my responsibilities as a father and to enjoy my son.

But each of these people probably has hidden goals, too. They might include the following:

Child: To get some treats from my Dad. To torment my stepmother a little to get even with her for taking my Dad away from Mom and me.

Mother: To give myself some free time. To make *him* share the responsibility of raising *our* kids.

Father: To ease my guilt over leaving my family.

I think it helps if everyone recognizes not only his good motives, but his more selfish ones as well. We might not need to spell them all out to each other, but we should recognize them so that we can responsibly control them. Visiting shouldn't be used as an opportunity to hurt and antagonize each other.

3. *Set up visits to permit all of the participants to meet their needs as much as possible.* The last phrase is important, because what is possible is necessarily limited, and meeting needs is an easily distorted goal. Imagine a situation in which a chronically hospitalized mother has children being raised by foster parents under the supervision of an agency. The mother's psychiatrist may insist that the mother needs visits with her children; the foster parents may counter that they need freedom from the disruptions her visits cause the family.

The agency caseworker may argue that the children need to see their mother so that they can learn to accept the fact that she isn't able to care for them. All of these needs may be genuine, but no single plan can meet them all perfectly. It will take a cooperative spirit to settle on a compromise, a plan that may have to be revised several times, with such details as place, time, and length of visits altered so that everyone can live with the plan and its limited satisfaction of needs.

4. *Make sure visits are planned.* I have been referring to a plan all along, which might seem strange to you, or hard to understand. I am talking about a written statement which spells out to all of the participants the circumstances under which visiting will take place. The next paragraphs will deal with the details of a plan. The written plan may seem somewhat artificial and lacking in spontaneity, but it helps to eliminate unnecessary conflicts over visiting, to assure that visiting has positive goals, and to ensure that visiting is not destructive for any of the participants. Writing out a plan helps you anticipate likely questions and problems and lets you handle them in a context of reason. Remember that it is never too late to make a plan. If you are presently involved in a visiting arrangement which does not have the elements mentioned in this chapter, take the initiative to work out a good plan.

Set up a good visiting plan. As you draw up your plan, keep the following points in mind.

1. *A good visiting plan is specific.* When we talk about a visiting plan, we sometimes mean an overall arrangement for contact between the child and his family, and we sometimes mean the specifics of a particular Saturday afternoon. A good visiting plan provides guidelines for both. Naturally, when visiting first begins the latter kind of details must have a prominent place. As visiting continues, the people involved will learn to handle these details more spontaneously, but at first almost everything may need to be written down. Start your plan by answering five basic questions.

- Who will be there? Consider everyone—right down to the family dog. Will the dog help ease tension, or will he terrify one of the children? Are you supposed to sit in? What if one child says at the last minute that he wants to do something else? The plan should stipulate who will be present.

• Where will the visit take place? At your home? The park? The movies? A shopping mall? Another home?

• What are the time limits? When will the visit begin, when will it end, and how often will it occur?

• What are the transportation arrangements?

• What will take place during the visit?

If the visiting plan includes more than person-to-person contact, you need to provide additional specifics. If the contact is a phone call, are you to listen in? Will you set a time limit? If the contact is a gift, may it be something you have forbidden the child to own? Some of these details may seem very trivial in advance, but they are just the kind of details which, when left unresolved, may spoil a visit for everyone.

2. *A good visiting plan has clearly spelled-out goals.* These may be both general or long-term goals and limited or short-term goals. The more agreement there is about long-term goals, the less need there is to be specific about the goals of a particular series of contacts. In some cases it works best to establish and meet short-term goals first, and then establish long-term goals. To illustrate: You are caring for an infant while her teenage mother gets her own life in order and learns how to care for her child. An immediate goal of a particular visit might be that she learn how to bathe her child. If the mother meets this and other similar short-term goals, you can realistically establish the long-term goal that the mother maintain contact with her child. You can think of similar illustrations.

3. *A good visiting plan makes room for gradually increasing involvement between parent and child, for growth in their relationship.* In a very tense situation in which a child has been taken away from abusive parents, the first contact possible might be only a brief phone call. The mother might simply ask you about her child without requesting to speak to her, maybe sending a "hello to Mary" through you. But if the contact is successful, the next contact should permit a greater degree of

intimacy—perhaps the mother could say hello to Mary herself. The contacts should continue to progress if they are successful, but you should also provide for "backing up" to less intense encounters—without hassle or recriminations. Here's another example: Perhaps the child's parents are dead, and you have never talked with him about the accident in which they were killed. If so, it would be inappropriate to suddenly launch into a 15-minute discussion of all the details after dinner one night. Instead, try making a quiet reference to a current event. You might say, "When I see a story in the paper about an accident involving kids, I think of your mother and I feel sad." Your statement calls for no particular response, but it lets the child know that you do think of his parent, and that it is O.K. for him to remember her and mention her if he wants to. You can move on gradually from there, guided by his readiness to discuss the subject.

4. *In a good visiting plan, all of the participants usually know the guidelines.* In the case just cited, you may have a plan for acquainting a child with his past, a plan which you do not spell out to him. But in general, when a visiting plan involves some kind of physical contact, all of the parties involved should participate in making the plan, have a copy of the plan, and be allowed to suggest changes in it. Even a very young child should be included. If he can't read, he can certainly understand your explanation of the plan. Give him a copy of the plan, too; it gives him a sense of responsibility and control in his situation, something even a very young child can need. He should not be left to feel that things "just happen" to him, that he has no control over his life.

5. *A good visiting plan provides for evaluation and changes.* All of the people who participate in making and carrying out a visiting plan should be involved in deciding how well its goals are functioning. The evaluative process is another thing that should be spelled out in the plan. In evaluation, it is a good thing to remember that a contact is not bad simply because it causes discomfort, or because it is inconvenient, or because it doesn't work miracles. Try answering the following questions to gauge the worth of a visit.

- Did the visit serve some of its goals, at least in part? For instance, in the example used earlier, the question would be this: Did the young mother have a pleasant visit with her baby, and did she learn to bathe him?

• If the visit caused stress or unhappiness, was it manageable? Sometimes a child wets the bed after a parental visit, or a mother feels very sad when she leaves her child. Can you cope with these consequences?

• Will changing specifics improve the visits? For example: the child's bedwetting is not necessarily an emotional reaction to his parent's visit. The visit might just have made him too physically tired to function typically—or he may simply have had too many cans of pop. Remember that everything that happens after a visit isn't necessarily an emotional consequence of it. Maybe as simple a thing as limiting the child's intake of liquids could solve the problem.

• What is the next step in the plan, and are we ready for it?

In summary, a good plan is specific, goal-directed, and flexible; it is known to all parties and provides for evaluation and change. If you sit down with others involved to try to work out the visiting plan together, you will find yourselves asking certain common questions. Other parents' general answers to them might be helpful to you.

How frequent should the visits be? Assess your particular situation to find out. Remember that a very young child has a short memory, so frequent brief visits will mean more to him than occasional longer visits. Daily visits might be best if you are caring for a child whose mother will soon take him back home. Another consideration is the extent to which the visits upset the child's routine, place a strain on a working parent with transportation difficulties, and so forth. If, after a trial period, all of the parties involved are reasonably satisfied with visiting frequency, it is probably right.

Where should the visit take place? I will outline some of the advantages and disadvantages of at-home visits and away-from-home visits. Try applying these factors and others to your particular situation to determine which visit will work best for you—or if you will benefit most from a combination of the two.

In general, a visit in the child's present home is less disturbing to him. The process involved in getting ready to go some place, going, returning, and then settling in again is exciting and tiring, especially for a young child. The actual visit may be overshadowed by all of the other parts of the process. If the visit is in the child's home, it is also less likely to be cancelled because of bad roads, a cold the child has gotten, school conflicts, and so forth. If the child is visited in his home, it is also easy and natural for him to bring out school papers, to find a game to play, or to get some help on a school assignment. The visiting parent can then keep in touch with his child's ordinary routine more easily, and fit more naturally into the child's life.

If the visit takes place in the child's home, it is also less likely that your other children will see it as a special treat which they must miss. Your children could become resentful if the parent drops by your house and "favors" the new child with a trip to the movies or a shopping spree. This resentment might interfere with their acceptance of the new child. Of course this is only one consideration; don't be unduly swayed by it.

Also keep in mind that visits outside the home are sometimes overly stimulating to the child. The visiting parent quite often falls into the role of provider of exciting presents and opportunities. The goal, of course, is that he be a parent, not Santa Claus or a tour guide. Too much activity may leave too little time for talking or any other form of real communication.

Of course, at-home visiting has disadvantages, too. The most serious disadvantage is that the visiting parent does not feel very comfortable there, as a rule. For various reasons, the atmosphere may be strained if the adults who care about the child are together. The child feels this strain and naturally enjoys the visit less. Another potential problem of at-home visiting is that the parent and child might not be able to talk freely, or might not know how to spend their time together. One visiting mother once told me that having her child's other mother there gave her child the idea that it was unsafe for the two of them to be alone together. Discomfort like this can shorten visits, and both the child and the parent often benefit more from longer visits.

In making the decision about the visiting place, I think the most important goal is to make the visit a natural, fairly low-key part of the child's life. And wherever it takes place, the visit should promote the goals of the visiting plan.

Be a good visiting parent. With these general ideas in mind, I will give specific suggestions for making visits successful. Keep in mind that in this section I will be talking to the *visiting* parent.

Visits with the pre-school child. Many of these visits will probably take place in the child's present home. As the visiting parent you may want to join in whatever the child usually does at that time of day. Or you may plan to make your visit coincide with the child's supper and bath time, so that you can supervise these activities. To establish continuity, try reading a story to be continued or re-read on the next visit. Sometimes you might just sit and watch your child play; you don't need to constantly interact with him to make your visits interesting and productive. Your child may enjoy going on a short walk, or playing on the swings at a nearby playground. But don't feel compelled to be an entertainer during these visits. Cuddling the child while you watch Sesame Street together or rocking him to sleep may strengthen your relationship more than an activity-filled visit. As a general rule the visits to the pre-school child should be short, unless much of the time you are simply "around" and not actively involved with your child. Too much close attention followed by periods without contact may confuse your child.

If your child is going to visit your home, concentrate on preserving his usual routines. It is usually best to continue nap times and serve familiar meals at familiar times. If these routines are disrupted, the child may become cranky and make the visit uncomfortable for everyone. If he goes home in an unpleasant mood, the visiting agreement might be strained. Because the pre-school child has difficulty handling prolonged excitement, special excursions should be simple and infrequent. A trip to see the fire engine is an exciting enough adventure to a four-year-old; he doesn't need a day-long visit to an amusement park.

Visits with the middle-years child. Because of his more

retentive memory and his ability to accept routine, the middle-years child can adapt better to a regular visiting plan. He is better able to explain what he enjoys, when it is best for you to come, and how he would like your visits to fit into his life. Following are some suggestions for things to do together—suggestions again based on the premise that a parent should not be an entertainer but a companion interested in developing a good long-term relationship with his child.

Consider activities—often commonplace ones—that will enrich his experience. The family the child is living in can probably suggest some that would be particularly good for him. Take your child through a car wash, to the zoo, to see trains or planes come in, on a ride on the city bus, or to a local museum. Children who are exposed to a wide variety of these kinds of experiences find reading more interesting and enjoyable, so make sure he has a library card, and show him how to check out books. Visit the "Y" together and try out their facilities, or try any other special program your community provides for children his age. Take him with you to your office and show him what you do; visit other businesses if possible. The idea is not to provide your child with excitement, but with background information about his community and the world that he will find interesting and useful. These activities will increase your conversational topics, too.

A similarly enriching group of activities are those that help him increase his skills and determine his values. For instance, plan to take your child on a picnic. But help the child plan the menu and shop for the food within a budget. Teach her how to build a fire and how to cook the food (or let her show you). Buy a new game you think looks like fun and learn to play it together, or let him teach you how to play one he likes. Do some work together at your home; teach him the skills he needs to really help you do it well. Let her cook dinner for you at your place. Ask him to help you with the Saturday chores at your house, then watch the football game on TV. Try teaching what are traditionally called "opposite sex" skills. Perhaps your girl would like to learn to throw a ball better, or maybe your son needs to learn to wash a load of clothes. Make arrangements to do some volunteer work together; the March of Dimes or the Cancer Fund would probably take you on as a team to do some collecting for them. In fact, fund drives and similar volunteer activities occur almost every month, and workers are always needed.

Another group of possible activities include the basic "child maintenance" activities often left exclusively to the child's "daily" parents. Plan to take him the next time he has to visit the dentist (share his worry ahead of time and his relief afterward). Take him to buy the new gym shoes he needs; volunteer to help out regularly with his scout troup or club. Perhaps you have a special skill you could demonstrate to such a group. Your child will be especially glad to have his friends see that he has "regular" parents.

Even if it makes you uncomfortable, I think you should sometimes visit your child in his present home. You will get a better idea of what life is really like for him if you spend some time in the place where he is living. The first few times will probably be strained, but if you have a definite idea of what you are going to do, that will help. Take along a puzzle to work as you talk, or offer to come and help him mow the lawn or wash the car if that is his job. You also will want to make some visits to his school. His teachers and others will appreciate your interest and cooperation, and it will improve your child's life at school.

Keep in mind that your goal is normal parent-child interaction, not entertainment. Of course you want your activities to be pleasant—but primarily because you're enjoying each other's company, not because you're doing exciting things. Whether your child is a first grader or a teenager, he needs you as a parent to help him make sense out of the world in which he lives.

Visits with the adolescent. During the adolescent years, a fundamental change takes place in visiting arrangements. The effectiveness of visits depends almost entirely on the adolescent. If he is cooperative, wants the visits, and enjoys them, almost any plan can be made to work. But if he doesn't cooperate, nothing will work, although he can be forced to go through the motions of a successful visit. Certainly many of the activities mentioned before can be continued, but as you maintain a relationship with your adolescent, try to respect his increasing independence and his need to divide his time between you and his peers—and, possibly, the demands of a job. Remember, too, that his growing awareness of moral choice may make him highly critical of you in your choices, especially as they affected his life. Try not to argue with him or engage in self-justification. State your reasons for your decisions calmly, and give him the freedom to evaluate them. With increasing maturity he will come to understand more of the constraints and failures of adulthood. If he rejects your attempts to continue the relationship, do not retaliate by rejecting him. Continue whatever support you can, maintain whatever contacts are possible, and wait out this period of reevaluation on his part.

If your visiting is going to work, you need to avoid certain traps. One I have already mentioned: don't let the child get into the habit of thinking of you as an entertainer. Two: avoid criticizing his current situation, the clothes he is wearing, the lifestyle of his present family. Three: don't be defensive about your situation. Both of you can learn to accept what must be. Enjoy your visits.

Avoid playing the sabotage game. The most important key to a successful visiting plan is determination on the part of all parties to make it work. Any participant in the plan has the power to foul it up. Sometimes sabotage is deliberate; sometimes the participants seem unaware that their actions are undercutting their verbal agreements and good intentions. I could write a book-long list of methods of sabotage without exhausting all the possibilities; the following are only the more common forms of it. Even if all parties involved seem to be cooperating, look for subtle signs of sabotage if you're having trouble with your plan.

Sabotage! Make the child upset right before the visit is scheduled to start. For instance: Announce that all homework must be done before the visit begins. If he is anxious about the visit or especially anticipating it, he may be in no emotional state to get the work done well, or get it done at all. Then you can complain loudly, he can yell and slam his books around, and in the middle of this full-fledged uproar, his visitor will arrive. How can anyone argue with your noble purpose to see that he does his schoolwork and gets a good education? A mere visit has to be less important than his education, doesn't it? Solution: Recognize that this was a poor way to start the visit and a poor way to get the homework done, and change your scheduling of demands. If visits are habitually preceded by an uproar, analyze why and do something constructive about it.

Sabotage! Put on the dog, work a subtle "put-down" into the conversation, or in some other way make the visitor feel uncomfortable enough so that he won't visit again. Visiting may put a great emotional strain on the visiting parent, especially at first, and a little added stress imposed by you may be enough to make him give up. Then you can say, "I tried, but he just never came through." If you hear yourself saying this, take an honest look at your own behavior. Did you encourage or discourage him?

Sabotage! Devise frequent last-minute emergencies so that visits don't occur as planned. Any member of the plan can play, even the children. When visits are cancelled—particularly if they are cancelled frequently—you should examine those "emergencies." What was the *real* reason behind the cancellation?

Sabotage! Use visits to continue a war. Fight with your husband or wife, and divide the family into camps. If one parent ends up with the children, and the other ends up with the visiting parent, the war may be continued: the children and the visiting situation are the ammunition. This is dirty pool. Find another way to handle the unresolved conflict, and don't use the children as weapons in adult wars.

Sabotage! Choose the visiting time to get into a highly charged discussion about some other part of the relationship. For instance: If the parent is behind on child support payments, you may grab at this opportunity to confront him about it. The unpleasant feelings and bitter discussion likely to develop may carry over into the visit and ruin it. Solution: Write a letter explaining the problem. Or make an appointment to discuss it at another time. In any case, don't use the child to get at the parent you think is behaving irresponsibly.

Sabotage! Ask prying questions after the visit, disguising them as "evaluative" questions. Sometimes a restructured family seems to want the child to complain about the visit. Encouraging this not only spoils the visit, but may eventually backfire: the child may come to resent your negative probing. If the child is reluctant to talk about a visit afterward, he probably has picked up some signals from you—either that you don't want to hear about it, or that you will respond negatively to everything he says. Solution: Show a positive interest in the visit and a willingness to discuss it. Let the child know that you want him to enjoy time spent with his biological parent. Remember that if he feels pressured to completely separate his relationships with the two of you, his closeness to both of you will suffer.

Sabotage! For at least a week after the visit, blame it for every problem you have with the child. Sometimes visits are followed by behavior that distresses you. We have already discussed the need to evaluate this behavior as a possible indicator of the visit's success. But it is sabotage to blame *every* behavior you don't like on the visits. You may complain that after visits he wets the bed or gets into more fights at school. But is the correlation real or imagined? You complain that he is very sassy when he comes home from a visit. But are you actually provoking some of that sassiness as an excuse to punish him because you are jealous of his joy in the visit? Are you saying things like, "Just because you get away with that with your mother, don't think you can do it around me"? Such statements invite bad behavior by implying both a criticism of the mother and a threat.

Visiting brings up all of the ambivalent feelings and many of the ambivalent situations that are involved in raising a child not your biological own. That makes the situation ripe for sabotage. But remember that the goals of visiting are too important to let sabotage destroy them.

How to be a Good "Weekend Parent"

Some custody arrangements involve more than visits of a few hours. A teenager may spend every other weekend and specified vacation periods with his biological parent. Two preschool children may spend every weekend with their father because that is when he can be home to care for them. Such arrangements are usually referred to as "visiting," but the time involved and the character of the arrangement are not described very well by that word. Confusion over the nature and purpose of these extended visits sometimes creates problems.

It is important to remember that the goal of the contact is the most important factor in this situation. The primary reasons that the child is spending time with this adult are basically the same as those reasons for briefer visits. But the more time involved, the more important it is that the setting and the relationship be everyday—constant in many ways. If, instead, a host-guest relationship develops, many problems also develop. The frequent visitor becomes bored with the "entertainment," and the "host" or "hostess" often begins to resent the unappreciative houseguest. If you are a child's biological parent, it helps if both of you think of you as the parent—not the entertainer—when you are together. Following are some specific suggestions that might help you—particularly if you are a "weekend parent."

1. Establish rules for the household. Because the child is not a guest, but a member of your family for the time he stays with you, he should obey family rules, or adaptations of them. Sometimes a parent or step-parent decides to settle rules by stating, "This is my home, and while you're here, we'll do things my way." This is better than having no rules at all, but it does not meet the goal of a parent-child relationship; it makes the child an outsider. Instead of imposing rules. ask the child for cooperation by saying, "I realize that in your other home you have certain ways of doing things. But we have special ways of doing things here, too. We need to work out some kind of compromise while you're here." You may have to be quite firm—especially at first—about enforcing the rules you agree upon, but if a child has helped make the rules he will be more willing to abide by them. (The chapter on discipline in the functional family offers suggestions for effective rule-making.)

2. Establish basic routines for each visit. Establishing routines for visits will reduce exhaustion, tension, and general wear and tear on everyone. Routines should be flexible, yet constant enough to suggest stability. For instance, young children should have established times and places for taking naps if they usually nap during the day. If an extra room has to be converted into a bedroom each time the child comes, help him establish a routine to ready it, then to restore it to its regular use before he leaves. Regularly washing the dishes or doing some other daily chore helps the child realize that his stay with you isn't a vacation but a regular part of his life. The predictability of such routines also helps the child to adjust more quickly to the transition from home to home.

3. Develop some traditions and rituals to share. Difficulties often arise because each family wants the child to be with them on particular holidays, on his birthday, and so forth. With willingness and determination, you can get around these difficulties and turn the special times you spend with your child into memorable occasions. Maybe you can celebrate his birthdays every half-year instead of every full year; perhaps you can celebrate the day of his baptism instead of the day of his birth. If she can't be there for Christmas, why not celebrate St. Nick's Day each year. Make up your own family holiday if necessary, and celebrate it annually. If a day is given a special name and observed regularly with rituals you and your child create together, it can come to have great meaning in both of your lives. Whatever you do, emphasize what you share rather than what you are missing in his life. (Be sure to read "Providing for Family Unity and Individuality" in Chapter 5.)

4. Maintain a natural activity level. Don't wear your child out with excessive "doing." If he goes back home exhausted after visiting you, he will not be well-prepared to resume his life in his other home. If you are exhausted, too, you will have a similar problem. Certainly you will want to share some special times that may be a little taxing; he has occasional "big days" with his other family, too. But most visits should be low-keyed, leaving you and the child refreshed and ready for your usual activity. On Monday it should be back to school for him, back to work for you—after a pleasant but not frantically busy time together.

If you are already following most of this chapter's suggestions and your visits are not going well, you need to re-assess the visiting arrangement you have developed. Perhaps you or the child has outgrown what was once satisfactory. For instance, a pre-school child who begins attending kindergarten will need a different arrangement. Similarly, a single parent who remarries may need a revised plan.

Watch for clues which suggest that your arrangement needs reworking. One clue may be tensions that develop because weekend visits interfere with school. An older child may have teachers who expect him to do homework on weekends. If the child is staying with you, maybe he can't get to the library or doesn't have the other resources he needs to get his work done. Or he may neglect his homework without your knowing it, because you are unaware of his assignments. He may hate going back to school on Monday because he is behind, yet not know how to get around the problem. His other parent may be nagging him about his homework and re-senting you for not seeing that it gets done. Another common problem develops if the child feels left out of school-related social and athletic activities that occur on weekends. He may become resentful because his visits with you some-times interfere with his social life, which is becoming increas-ingly important to him. If you realize that your visiting ar-rangement is creating this problem, be sure to make some positive changes.

Other tensions may develop because the child's presence on weekends interferes with your social life. American social life tends to be arranged around the weekend. But sometimes an adult finds himself unable to accept invitations or attend community events on weekends because his child is coming to visit. Either he is unable to get a babysitter, or he feels that he shouldn't go off and leave the child when they have so little time to spend together as it is. The weekend arrangement may be outdated. Maybe the parent made it when he was newly divorced, but now finds it restrictive because he has re-married and has resumed a more active social life. Compro-mises and changes are obviously in order. A good question to begin with is this: Does the visit always need to occur on the weekend?

Tensions can also develop if the parent-child relationship

becomes too central in the life of either adult or child. This
may sound impossible when you consider the relatively small
amount of time involved, but it can happen. Actually, a working couple with two teenagers does not spend the whole
weekend with the children, nor do either children or parents
plan their entire lives around spending the weekend together.
Yet a parent who has a child living with another family may do
just that, giving almost too much attention to the relationship and thus distorting its importance. Usually a child gradually becomes less dependent on the parent, and the parent
permits the child to spend an increasing amount of time on his
own. This development is perfectly normal—a fact which the
parent must accept and use to alter visiting arrangements if
that seems necessary. "I can't take a job because I have to go
see my Dad two weekends a month" means more to a teenager than the loss of a few dollars. It means sacrificing his
need for increasing independence. Make sure you let your
child grow up; adapt your visiting plans to give him the
freedom he needs.

Sometimes guilt over leaving the child in another person's
care or anger about a custody arrangement continues to get in
the way of productive visiting arrangements. These problems
are beyond the scope of this book, but they are certainly important; an adult plagued by them should get help to solve them.

Parent-against-parent competition can also cause
tension. You may be competing without being aware of it. Ask
yourself these questions: "Do I feel I have to be a better parent
than the other adult? Do I make comparisons between the
way *they* do things and the way *we* do things? Am I bribing the
child with nicer presents, more attention, better trips—all to
get him to agree that I treat him better than they do?" Whenever there is ongoing contact, competition can become a problem, and the child usually spots it quickly. It may make him
unhappy, silent, and defensive, or he may use it to manipulate both adults. Don't compete; let what you do complement
the benefits your child receives from the other family. Dis-
ruption in the structure of his life has cost him something.
With effort and imagination you can compensate for that in
many ways, but those compensations should be designed not
to win his approval or affection, but to enrich his life and
yours.

CHAPTER 5

MEETING SPECIAL CHALLENGES

The restructured family has all of the joys and difficulties of any other family. But it also has special problems and unique opportunities because of its special make-up. In this chapter are some suggestions for successfully meeting some of the special challenges that a restructured family may face.

Developing the Child's Self-esteem

Often a child who joins a restructured family has a very poor opinion of himself. This poor opinion is often called a poor self-concept, or lack of self-esteem. It may show itself in the child's refusal to try to adapt to his new family and his new school; in an exaggerated swagger or bragging; in tall tales about material possessions or exploits in his old home; or in a depressed or listless attitude. His theme song may be "I can't"—or it may be "I can do anything better than anybody."

It is very important to the child's future and his present well-being that he develop confidence in himself and his ability to contribute to others. To develop self-esteem, the child needs four things:

- A sense of belonging.
- A sense of competence.
- A sense of worth.
- A sense of meaning.

The sense of belonging grows out of the child's feeling that he is an important part of his family. A baby is given unconditional love: he is supplied with what he needs and is expected to give nothing in return. But gradually he has opportunities to give as well as take, and what he gives is welcomed. His ability to give, to care, is shaped by those who primarily care for him. A child usually perceives his family as his primary "care giver" because they give him verbal and physical expressions of love, and because they discipline him firmly and consistently and thoughtfully, paying attention to his age and other characteristics.

If a child feels he "belongs" to his biological family, leaving them can damage his self-esteem. If a child never felt part of his biological family, his self-concept will certainly be damaged. Whatever the background of the child who joins your family, try to give him the kinds of experiences that will make him feel he belongs. I have mentioned some already: designating an area in the house as his private space; giving him regular chores to do that make a needed contribution to family life; freely expressing love for him; disciplining him consistently; giving him a regular place at the dinner table. Be thoughtful and imaginative as you think up ways to demonstrate to him that he is part of your family.

The security of belonging gives the child the confidence he needs to function in the world. His self-concept thus begins to rest on competence, too. He sees himself as a worthwhile person not just because he belongs to someone, but also because he can do worthwhile things. Perhaps your new child is not as competent as he should be, and his inadequacies make him afraid to try things. Here are some steps you can take to encourage him.

1. *Don't do for him what he can do for himself.* You will need patience and self-control if he is inept, but remember that he'll learn best by *doing.*

2. *Don't overtask and discourage him.* Try to match challenges to his ability so he can succeed frequently.

3. *Limit your criticism.* You do not need to praise everything he does, such as poor work; he knows you are not sincere if you do. But do balance your criticism with plenty of encouragement and praise. Display the behavior you want him to develop: give yourself a verbal pat on the back when you do something well so that he learns it is O.K. to praise himself. Teach him complimentary words that he can use to praise himself and other family members.

4. *Learn to break into manageable segments the large tasks he needs to learn* so you can praise and reward his successful completion of every part. For instance: You think your new daughter could learn to set the table attractively, but she may not be able to absorb all of the how-to's in a single task-learning session. Divide the task into parts: fixing flowers for the centerpiece, folding the napkins, adding the silverware in the right places, and so forth. As she masters one part, praise her, and gradually increase the parts of the task she is responsible for as she succeeds at them. Success leads to further success; failure tends to further discourage a child with a poor self-concept.

5. *Help him handle his incompetency.* Don't say, "You can't do this because you're too little"; say instead, "Maybe you can't do it now, but you'll be able to do it when you're bigger." To encourage him, point out all of the things he can do now that used to be too hard for him. Try saying things like, "You can read now. Remember when. . ." or "You can think about economics now. Remember when that was just a big word to you?" or "You can throw a ball and catch it. Remember when we had to roll it to you?" Remembering how much he has learned and is learning will make him confident that he can learn much more as he grows.

6. *Teach him to talk positively to himself.* Words have a powerful effect, including those we say to ourselves.

7. *If the child has trouble with schoolwork, try to arrange to get him extra help as soon as possible.* Sometimes a child can get special help at school, but being singled out this way may further embarrass or depress the child. It might be best to arrange instead for a private tutor, or to have an encouraging person help him at home. Teenagers now work in planned programs to help children develop confidence in their learning skills, an experience that is good for both the children and the teenagers.

8. *Consider arranging for him to take lessons in a sport or another activity that interests him.* Perhaps he could learn to swim, to play chess well, or to play the guitar. His new skill may increase his sense of competence and positively affect other areas of his life.

A sense of worth also positively influences the child's self-concept. Worth comes from knowing that you are more than a thing—that you are a creature of God with value and purpose. For many adults, their sense of worth depends on their ability to produce, to accomplish. Because children often feel quite unproductive, they sometimes feel quite useless. We need to teach them a less functional sense of their value. In addition, we need to recognize the other ways in which our culture devalues children. They are regarded as expensive, or in the way, or as impediments that keep adults from living their own lives. Try to let your children know that you are glad you have them. Enjoy them. They will develop a sense of worth from the fact that you, a capable, caring adult, spend time with them and feel that parenting them is worthwhile.

Especially during adolescence, a child's self-concept is shaped by a sense of meaning. The teenager asks, "Why do I exist? Why am I doing what I am doing?" Sometimes he becomes impatient with imperfection. "I can't be perfect so I might as well quit" is his typical response to his idealistic desire for perfection. He needs help in coming to terms with the imperfections of the world, and encouragement to keep trying. The adolescent may also be frustrated by a recent realization that moral choice is not a black-and-white matter, as he thought when he was younger. Let him know that moral choice is often difficult for you, too, and be willing to listen without passing judgment as he verbalizes his struggle to make good moral choices.

A child's self-concept is particularly fragile at certain times. I have already mentioned that joining a new family can upset a child. The death of a loved one can also wound him. Other difficult periods are age-related. Junior high is a particularly hard time for a child with a poor self-concept. Even a child with a good self-concept might suffer temporarily. The young teenager's need to belong may conflict with his intense need to be independent. Often he appears to solve this problem by joining a close-knit peer group (a gang or a clique). A child's self-concept might also suffer at this time because of his struggle with competence: at this age a child often overestimates his skills and then fails, and adults often underestimate his skills and make him feel incompetent.

Fortunately, you can help your teenager improve his self-concept. Try encouraging him to participate in a variety of extracurricular activities so that he can feel competent in one or more of them. He might also benefit from holding a job, even a voluntary unpaid one. Remember that society insensitively attacks his sense of worth. Think about the cartoon of a junior high student; it is usually quite negative. He is hit from all sides by insensitive questions ("How can anyone stand to teach junior high?") and critical assessments ("He's at that gawky, pimply age"). You can counteract some of this by explaining to him what is happening to him physically (see the chapter on goals and development), and by generously expressing your love for him and his worth to you. Let him be independent, but make sure you continue to nurture his sense of belonging to your family—something he needs very much. Try to discourage people from saying things like, "He is so lucky you were willing to take him on at that age." Make it clear to him that you believe you both are lucky to have each other.

Psychologists and others have thoroughly studied the development of a positive self-concept. Many good books on the subject, some written particularly for parents, are available at libraries and bookstores.

Handling Special Emotional Problems

Even the most carefully managed household suffers strains and tensions. In addition, children are born with varying degrees of inherited ability to handle the normal difficulties of life. Most children and their parents successfully cope with these problems; one problem of growing up is usually forgotten as another challenge replaces it. But children who enter the functional family are often less resilient because many of them have endured unusual stress and strain. They may have been living with adults who couldn't provide for their physical or emotional needs. Or perhaps they are coming to you because some kind of tragedy struck their other family. Maybe their parents fought constantly and finally divorced bitterly; maybe one parent became sick and died; maybe both parents were killed in a car accident.

In these situations children may develop patterns of response which help them survive this trauma but which are not healthy for them in the long run. Some of these problems

can be handled quite easily, but others will require professional help. I will discuss some common problems, suggest how
families can handle them, and indicate when getting outside
help would be wise.

Eliminating causes of emotional problems. Emotional
problems can often be solved if you handle their underlying
causes skillfully.

Separation anxiety. Every child who moves from one home
to another feels some separation anxiety. The more frequently he has had to be moved in the past, the less control he has
felt he had over these moves; and the more abrupt the present
move to your home, the more likely it is that his adjustment
will be difficult. Your child may show any one of a variety of
symptoms. He may be exceedingly cold and aloof, protecting
himself from another possible rejection by refusing to get involved with you. He may be very tensely obedient, trying to
please you so he won't be sent away again. Or he may be
rough and aggressive and behave obnoxiously, trying to get
you to throw him out; this behavior makes him feel like he has
some control over the situation and can bring on the feared
rejection and get it over with. He might also regress in his
behavior: a seven-year-old may resume bedwetting, or a
twelve-year-old may have temper tantrums that resemble
those of a four-year-old.

The best remedy for separation anxiety is prevention, so I
will deal with prevention first (though I realize that it may be
too late for that in your situation). Following are the steps
which seem to help the child cope with the loss of one home
and the acceptance of a new one.

1. Give the child a transitional period. That is, let him
become as familiar as possible with your home and family
before he moves in. (The earlier chapters about getting acquainted with a new child and about visiting explain how to
make this a good experience.) Explain to the child what is happening; and be sure he knows he is not to blame for this move.

2. Let him take some of his past with him. Let him bring
familiar objects from his old home; whenever possible—
especially at first—let him do things the way he did them in his
old home. Often the "new" parents will buy a child new

clothes and new toys. In addition, the child must adapt to new foods, a new daily schedule, a new house, a new school, and other major changes. Understandably, all of these simultaneous changes can be unsettling. Your willingness to do things "the old way"—to let him keep his dirty old toys, to let the teenager dress in his familiar sloppy jeans and shirts—will help him adjust to his new home and may prevent more serious difficulties later.

3. *Let him know that he doesn't have to reject the people he is leaving.* Surprising as it may seem to an adult, a child does not necessarily realize that he can love a new person without giving up the old. This mistaken impression can be corrected if both the "old" parent and the "new" parent mutually encourage the child to love both of them. (Methods for doing this were discussed in the section about visiting in Chapter 4.) The child should not have to feel that separation is the same as total loss.

4. *Recognize that separation involves grief and that a period of mourning is perfectly normal.* Much helpful material has been written lately about the process of grief. Elisabeth Kübler-Ross has delineated the stages of healthy grief: denial, anger, bargaining, depression, and acceptance. Maybe your child is going through one of these stages; realizing this may help you to accept his behavior and work through the period with him. But we should remember that the expression of grief is a uniquely personal thing, shaped partly by personality and partly by cultural and familial influence. We should not insist that every person cope with his grief in a particular way. For instance, if your teenager refuses to talk about his feelings about moving, you should not necessarily label his behavior as "denial" and see it as a problem. He may be dealing with the facts in a very personally satisfactory way—he just might not be the kind of person who "talks it out."

What should you do if moving the child into your home was an awkward or painful process, and now the child is having trouble adapting to his new home? As much as is possible, try to follow the four suggestions for prevention above. It is never too late to do some of them. Try also to express to your child your recognition that this process is painful to him. Reassure him that you stand between him and repetition of the pain, that you are not going to welcome him only to send him away. Be aware of the danger of rejecting this child in retaliation for the pain his behavior is causing you. Seek emotional support from other people so that you can continue to love this child who is not quite ready to return your affection.

Phobias. Phobias are unusual fears of normal situations, objects, animals, or other natural things; they are caused by emotional stress. A child might have a phobia about going to school, about dogs or cars—about almost anything. Get help for your child if he has a phobia that causes him or the rest of the family serious distress and inconvenience. Also get help if one phobia replaces another, a phenomenon which suggests that an underlying emotional problem remains. But remember that most phobias tend to go away by themselves, and that they are so common in children that they are considered normal. A teenage phobia, however, is apt to be more persistent, and may indicate a more serious emotional problem. Try to figure out the cause of the stress and eliminate or lessen it. If it persists and greatly hampers the child (if, for example, he can't go to school), get help from the family doctor, a school counselor, or a mental health professional.

Tics. This is the name we give to persistent, involuntary twitchings or movements of the body which have no physical cause. They may be more or less annoying to the child, but they usually bother other people more than the person who has them. Once again the cause is underlying tension, and the remedy is to seek out the source of the tension and lessen it. Frequent comments won't help, although occasionally an older child, if prompted, can learn to control a particular movement. Tics shouldn't unduly concern you: almost all children develop them at one time or another, and the vast majority go away by themselves.

Anxiety reactions. This is a general term used to describe unfocused fearfulness and tenseness. Unlike phobias, anxiety reactions have no specific trigger. In late childhood and early adolescence the child may feel dizzy and nauseous but be unable to explain the dread that makes him sick. These symptoms may be momentary or may last as long as a couple of hours. An older teenager may develop a more chronic, free-floating fear. He may complain of headaches, tiredness, and muscle tension, and an occasional wave of fear and panic. These reactions can be quite scary to both the adolescent and the parent. You can manage such reactions by pinpointing specific causes of the tension and eliminating them. The child or adolescent should know that his problem is triggered emotionally, not physically. A good physical examination might reassure him, particularly if he hasn't had one recently. Of course, if he undergoes a lot of tests, he may get worried; be sure to explain that you are only affirming his physical health. A teenager may prefer to explore his problem with a person other than a family member. If you get a professional to help him, be sure he does not think you are labeling him "sick" or "nuts."

Obessions and compulsions. An obsession is a tendency to think about something all of the time, such as thinking persistently about death. A compulsion is an insistence on repeating an action in a meticulously particular way. There is a good chance that obsessions will go away. Compulsions can range from mild, short-lived ones to very complicated, permanent rituals which take so much time that they prevent the child from getting anything else done. Explanations, reassurance, and lessening of stress in the child's life may help both of these problems. But if the problem persists and severely interferes with day-to-day living, the child should have professional help.

What else can you do? There are always two basic things you can do to help your child conquer his particular problem.

Provide good emotional models. The adults in some families have very unsatisfactory ways of handling emotional problems, and your new child may come from such a family. If so, it is possible that he is copying a parent's way of handling a problem. Our family once had a four-year-old who complained of a headache when he was asked to pick up toys, to eat a food he didn't particularly like, or to do certain tasks. It was obvious that he used the excuse of having a headache to avoid things he didn't want to do. I was not at all surprised to learn that frequently his mother went to bed with what she called a "sick headache." These headaches may have been genuine; regardless, the child saw headaches as a way to get out of an unpleasant situation, and in time probably would have developed genuine physical symptoms when he confronted such situations.

This example illustrates that adults need to be aware of how they handle problems, and try to be good models for their children. Children need to learn that all of us must cope with anger, unpleasant situations, things we are afraid of, unhappiness, and loneliness. Help your child become aware of feelings like fear and anger, and help him express them. Explain your feelings to him and show him how you deal with them in constructive ways. Perhaps you go for a walk when you're tense, or you visit a certain friend when you're discouraged. If your new child needs to learn better ways to cope with his emotions, perhaps he can adapt some of yours.

Interrupt negative cycles of behavior. To some extent, children's emotional problems can occur in cycles in which the parents participate. That's why a change in the adults' behavior might eliminate or improve the child's behavior problem. For example: A withdrawn child may have very demanding parents. The child withdraws at least partly because he does not feel he will ever be able to measure up to his parents' expectations. A fearful child may have overly anxious parents—the kind who always hover in the background issuing warnings and predicting catastrophe, either in words or actions. Eventually the child learns the messages so well that he issues constant warnings to himself even when the adults are not present. A demanding child (one who whines and complains, or one who is aggressive and prone to tantrums) may have overly solicitous parents. The more the parents try to please, the more demanding the child becomes. In your case, the child may have developed one of these behavior patterns before he joined your family, and you may be unconsciously responding in a way that he has come to expect. If you can become less demanding, or less anxious, or less solicitous, you may be able to break the cycle.

When should you seek help? A parent may have trouble deciding when he should get outside help in managing his child's emotional problem. Certain behaviors do indicate that a child may need professional help: withdrawal from other people, delinquent behavior, chronic unhappiness, irrational suspiciousness, preoccupation with his health, and an inability to accept his own sex or to be normally interested, for his age, in the opposite sex. If your child has one of these problems or is beset by phobias, tics, obsessions, or compulsions, ask three questions: How long has it been going on? How much is it interfering in the child's development? How much is it upsetting the whole family? If your answers suggest that the problem is persistent and serious, seek help. The section on working with professionals provides some additional information.

Working with Professionals to Help Your Child

Though our society assumes that parents have primary responsibility for child-rearing, it does provide a network of assistance. Most parents enlist the help of the school, the church, the family doctor, and so forth. Although this section is written specifically to parents, it is not intended to downgrade or minimize the efforts of these others who contribute to the child's development.

When a problem develops in a child's life, it is very easy for adults to spend a great deal of time and energy trying to decide who's to blame. This has at least two bad results—and probably several I haven't thought of. First, it tends to put "the accused" on the defensive. Second, effort that should be used to solve the problem is spent in fending off responsibility or thinking up excuses for what happened. The person leveling the blame may correctly perceive that a problem does exist and find a scapegoat; he may not see how his accusation contributes to the problem, or what he could do to solve it. All in all, everybody wastes time and energy, and the child remains unhelped. Let me explain an actual incident that illustrates this problem. It is an incident recounted by a school board member to prove his claim that "parents just don't care."

Several witnesses saw John, an eighth grader, throwing bricks through four plate glass windows at his school. The principal of the school called John's father and asked him to come to the school to discuss John's action. The father told the principal that he had spent eight miserable years in that school and that was enough—he was never going to set foot in it again. If the principal wanted to talk, he could come to see him. And that was that.

No matter how carefully the principal may have worded his request, the father certainly felt blamed for his son's action and became defensive. (Perhaps he was to blame and felt hurt and angry.) The principal decided the situation was hopeless with a father like that, and just collected from the insurance company. (Very likely he, as part of the "miserable school," also felt blamed for John's action and wanted to withdraw from the situation.) The results: John continued to be destructive and disruptive at school.

In such situations the professional or the parent must use skill to begin to remedy the situation. John's father obviously hated the school and had spent years throwing verbal bricks at it; his son copied him, but threw real bricks instead. Had the principal been willing to visit the home and begin to build some kind of bridge between the family and the school, perhaps John might have begun to value his chance to get an education. If John had been a foster child or an adopted son, the principal might not have had a chance to discover so easily the source of his hostility to the school. In this case, the parents' cooperation would have been even more important. If parents refuse to lend constructive help, others embroiled in the problem must work all the harder.

Such a situation clearly illustrates why you should avoid making accusations like "You'll never amount to anything, just like your father" or "Your mother was just lazy about school. Do you want to be like her and flunk?" Even try to avoid *thinking* them. Such statements have a way of becoming self-fulfilling prophecies.

Besides avoiding blame-leveling, parents who want others to help them must be willing to honestly discuss the situation with professionals involved. This is not particularly easy for us; we tend to feel that what goes on in our homes is our business. It is difficult to express our fears, hopes, and failures to a stranger. But willingness to give honest information to a teacher, counselor, doctor, or other professional is a necessity. Remember that trust is all-important; be sure to find someone in whom you have confidence to help you.

Do not be afraid to seek out someone else if you can't communicate well with the professional you have chosen, or if you're not getting the help you need. Not all professionals are equally skilled, nor are they equally at home with different kinds of problems or different personalities. If possible, express your difficulties openly to the professional with whom you are working, and ask him to suggest other people to help you.

I would like to add a note about testing. When a child develops a problem, the first suggestion is often that he take a series of tests to "evaluate the situation." If you agree, your child will probably undergo psychological tests, I.Q. tests, personality tests, physical tests, and other evaluations. These are one way of identifying a problem, and can often be valuable. But it is important to realize a few things about testing. First, the tests are being given at a very stressful time in your child's life—the fact that they are being administered in response to a problem is evidence of that. For this reason they may not accurately reveal your child's skills and competencies, and their results shouldn't be emphasized too heavily in long-range planning. Our family had a child living with us whose test scores showed that he had barely average intelligence. As an adult he proved to have above-average intelligence. Such examples abound. Second, the best tests are probably less conclusive than the evaluation of competent people who know their job and your child. If your child's teacher has an opinion that differs from test results, I would tend to value the teacher's opinion until it was proved wrong. Third, since what we believe about a child's ability has a powerful effect on his performance, we should accept the most positive evaluation we can get and thus give the child the best possible chance to succeed. Test results will probably not be that encouraging. Fourth, remember that, no matter how many tests are completed, they don't solve the problem. Too often the child takes a battery of tests, the professional makes a series of more or less specific recommendations, and the problem is filed away. It will be up to you, as parent, to be sure that the necessary recommendations are acted upon if that responsibility is not assumed by someone else in the situation.

Quite often parents develop an adversary relationship with professionals. If this happens, they can end up in a counterproductive situation, one in which the child and professional appear to side against them. One factor which seems to contribute to this problem is the lack of openness between all of the members involved. The child or adolescent requires the professional to promise that he will not divulge to the parents anything he says. In a well-meant attempt to secure the child's confidence, the professional agrees. Obviously, the situation is ripe for exploitation by the child. The parents feel left out; often the professional only talks to them through the child. As one father explained to me, "I feel all he wants me to do is pay the bills and ask no questions about his methods, ideas, or progress. I'm not used to accepting that kind of blind deal." Treatment methods vary, but personally I am leery of those methods which do not involve the whole family, or methods which isolate child from parents or parents from child. The child and his family need to solve their problems *together* so that they can live together more closely and harmoniously.

I am sympathetic with professionals who feel that parents sometimes are the primary cause of the problem because they don't care, or because they can't change. If a professional fails at sincere efforts to establish a good working relationship with a child's parents, then of course the child must be helped almost in spite of them. But I believe the professional should always assume at the outset that the parent does want good things for his child and can be helpful. When he assumes that the parents "don't care" or "won't change" or "blame everybody but themselves," he dooms his goal of a cooperative relationship before he begins. As parents, we must also assume that professionals working with our child—teachers, counselors, psychologists—also care, that they are trained to help and will also take responsibility for change. Belittling thoughts—"She's just in it for the pay"; "He doesn't know about kids because he never had any"; "The schools aren't doing their job"—just put up barriers that make it impossible to work together for the child's good.

In our very mobile society both families and professionals move often, so teachers, counselors, and others are not always familiar with every family's situation. But they usually need such background information to be truly helpful. Because you are trying to emphasize your child's identification with *your* family, you may be reluctant to give his family history to everyone who meets him. You probably need to strike some kind of balance. Of course, the experiences and relationships of his past are very much a part of his present, and in some cases the professionals might benefit from learning about them. On the other hand, if the child doesn't have serious problems, you might prefer that his past not be explored. In any case, you should reveal the history not to fix blame ("I didn't cause these problems—his first family did") but to give information that may help in analyzing and correcting the child's problem. For their part, professionals should be aware that new parents may be quite sensitive about revealing this information.

In the long run, the new parent must be willing to be identified with the new child and his behavior. I know from experience how unpleasant it is when my new child has a temper tantrum in the grocery store and I hear the whispered, "If that boy were my child. . .," and I get the disapproving looks. I want to shout, "He's not mine. I didn't make him like this." But the less others "accuse" people like us, the less defensive we'll be. In this situation, an offer to help, or a friendly smile and a comment like, "Grocery shopping is difficult with children, isn't it?" would be much more appreciated. In the same way, the parent and professional must concentrate on helping each other with the present, and on using the past as a tool to understand, not a weapon to punish.

If you are thinking about seeking help for your child or family, remember that counseling does not always need to be lengthy and expensive. We often have the misconception that only years of therapy at a cost of thousands of dollars will make any difference. Actually, many situations can be dramatically improved in a relatively short time, perhaps only six or eight weeks. Even a single objective talk with a skilled teacher or counselor may help a great deal. If you think cost is prohibitive, remember this: more and more communities are making professional counseling services available through churches, schools, clinics, and mental health centers. These programs are often funded in such a way that charges are based on family income.

Don't think you must wait until you have a serious "text-book" problem on your hands before you seek professional help. After all, you don't wait for double pneumonia to set in before you treat a child who has a cold. It's a welcome change for a counselor to hear about a problem while it is still in a relatively simple stage. If you don't know how to handle a situation and it is bothering you and disrupting relationships in your family, ask for help. Consult your family doctor or minister, or your child's teacher or school counselor. They will know who can help you if they are not equipped to help you themselves.

Coping with Failure

Human beings have to come to terms with failure; no one experiences unbroken success. In the task of parenting children not biologically our own, we must be prepared to deal with failure. What will we do if the child must be moved, if he doesn't "turn out well," if the relationship we build is less than we had hoped? We may have to face such outcomes despite our best efforts. Consider the following possibilities.

- You got along fairly well with your daughter, but the two of you were never close. When she got married she dropped you completely for her husband's family; in fact, you haven't seen her in months, although she lives nearby.

- You took in a teenage girl who probably was headed for girl's school. A year later you learn that she is four month's pregnant.

- A young boy joined your family and acted like a model teenager, but you have learned that he is persistently undermining the values you are teaching your twelve-year-old son. He has taught the twelve-year-old to smoke and organized him and two of his friends into a shoplifting trio.

- You thought you could accept someone else's child and you just can't. It's nothing about the little girl or her behavior. It's you, and you are disappointed in yourself. She is only six years old. How can you reject a little child? you scold yourself.

People I know have experienced these and many other kinds of parenting failures. I have experienced some myself. These might be called the big failures. They involve a disappointing and essentially permanent judgment about a long-term relationship with a particular child. Parents are also plagued by short-term failure. We go to bed at night feeling sad and discouraged because the whole day seems to have gone poorly, or because we blew up at a child and said things we never intended to say. Or we despair because the child is in serious trouble at school or has been caught shoplifting. On these nights, we feel like failures. What can we do? What can you do?

Define failure realistically. The first thing you may need to do is determine if you should be thinking in terms of failure. How much did you expect your child to change? Maybe your goals were too idealistic; maybe you need to reset them. What other things are influencing your child besides you, his parents? You cannot expect to have the only effect on him. Have you waited long enough for results? Many parents become discouraged when raising an older adolescent, because he seems hopelessly rebellious; yet ten years later, when he visits home with his own family, he has obviously adopted their lifestyle and values. You must also remember that a child is not a piece of plastic conforming to your mold; he is a person, responsible for contributing to his own development. Of course you will make some mistakes as you guide him—but your child will make some mistakes, too. You should take steps to correct your mistakes, but scolding yourself excessively isn't one of them. Following these suggestions might help.

Don't level blame. As I mentioned before, a problem with a child tempts us to find a scapegoat. This is non-productive: energy is wasted, people become defensive, and constructive actions get sidetracked. Of course you may need to determine who is responsible for certain actions that might contribute to the problem, but this should be done in a non-judgmental way.

Don't try to justify your actions. I have basically concluded that unless a person has himself raised a child not biologically his own, he has little idea of the factors involved. So if an unschooled observer wonders about some of your actions, don't be intimidated. You should not feel obligated to justify yourself, nor should you get cornered into criticizing your child's behavior. State the facts *if necessary* and let it go at that. Even though Ann Landers frequently advises it, we can't really go around telling people to mind their own business. But we can recognize prying and change the subject.

Talk it over with someone. Sometimes it is helpful to discuss your feelings of guilt and failure with another person who has had a similar experience. Frequently foster parents find other foster parents are the best people to talk to when things don't work out with a particular child, because almost all foster parents have had that happen. But be sure to choose someone who can help you overcome your feelings, not someone who will further depress you.

Be realistic about the role you play. A child is not just a product of his environment; he is shaped by heredity and his own personality, too. Since he chooses what he pays attention to, he may distort or overemphasize certain factors. Remember, too, that he helped create the environment which is now helping shape him: he responded to you just as you responded to him. And he probably has been affected by a previous environment and previous training. Even if you could erase that past, you could not create a perfect environment now. You are important in this child's life, but you are not all-important in either his successes or his failures.

Don't let society blame you. Our culture is very hard on parents. Bruno Bettelheim frequently reminds us that when he was young and a child got into trouble, the neighbors all said, "Poor Mrs. Jones. Her son is a black sheep." Now they say, "Poor John Jones. What a terrible family he must have." You may feel guilty about failing because society has made you responsible for the way your child "turns out." But remember that at any age the child is responsible, to some extent, for his own behavior, and certainly a young adult must accept responsibility for his actions. Try to strike a healthy balance: don't run from your part in failure, but don't take on another's responsibility, either.

In addition to applying the generalizations above, use the following specific suggestions for handling the situations that can send you to bed discouraged with the day.

1. *Contain the damage.* By this I mean that you should do what you can as soon as you can to keep the situation from getting worse. This may mean an apology, a trip to the school, or a talk with the child. Don't let the situation fester and get worse.

2. *Don't let the situation snowball.* (Snowballing is described in the chapter on discipline.) It is easy for a specific failure to get mixed up with other problems and grow.

3. *Don't generalize.* Don't say "I'm getting nowhere with this child" when the specific problem is a certain action. Try to talk about mistakes, yours or the child's, in specific terms. If you generalize, generalize about successes. And try to praise before you criticize. If your child has a problem at school, say something like, "You're usually polite to adults. Why did you yell at your teacher?" Avoid saying, "You're always getting into trouble with your big mouth."

4. *Retreat sooner next time.* If you blew up when you didn't mean to, or let a minor incident become a major one before you realized it, plan to behave differently next time. Figure out how you will avoid having the same thing happen again. Perhaps your spouse can handle it, or perhaps you can arrange to signal him or her to take over when you know you're losing control.

5. *Change what you can.* Correct your mistake if possible, and help the child correct his.

6. *Forget it.* No fair bringing it up the next time the child makes a mistake; and no fair hitting yourself over the head with your mistake again and again.

Avoid setting yourself up for failure. Particularly observe the following "don'ts."

Don't add a child to your family to replace a child you have lost. When the child comes, he should come for his own sake. Make sure you give yourself enough time to mourn. If you act too soon, any number of things may go awry. You may try to make the new child like the lost child, and he may not feel loved for himself. Or the painful memories and comparisons his presence provokes may prolong your grief. You might also inadvertently give this new child too much too soon—too much love and longing, too much attention. This intensity may actually prevent his gradually learning to love you and feel comfortable with you.

Don't plunge into a new situation without adequate preparation. (This point has been thoroughly made in earlier chapters.) If for some reason the child joined your family abruptly, try to build the foundation you need as soon as possible.

Don't try to do it all alone. Other parents, various professionals, adult brothers and sisters, and various community organizations can help you. Be sure to take advantage of them.

Learn from failure. If you handle your failures constructively, they can help you grow into a more mature person. They help to make you sensitive to your own weaknesses and those of others, to others' pain and sorrow. As you discover what helps you, you can learn how to help others more effectively. You can learn what it means to have your mistakes and failures forgiven, and how to offer that forgiveness to others.

Coping When a Child Leaves

Nothing is so painful for the functional family as losing a child whom they had hoped to keep. Less hard to bear but still painful is the loss of a child who has become part of the family but must move on according to plan. No matter how happy the expected outcome or how necessary the move, both the child and the family grieve over his leaving. In some ways it is like a death in the family, but there is no public mourning process nor much social support to help the family overcome its loss. That's why the family must work out its own ways of handling such moves, adapting them to each situation.

When I discussed separation anxiety earlier, I suggested ways to ease the child's transition from home to home. You may have the chance to follow these steps now, even if you couldn't follow them when the child first came to live with you. But before you prepare for the move, you and the other adults in the situation need to clearly understand why you are moving the child. Sometimes the stated reason is not the real reason, and assessing the situation honestly will make it better for all concerned. "For his own good" may be true, but if the whole truth includes the convenience or prejudices of some adults, that should be recognized. So should power plays in which a child is the pawn in a fight between adults. If the child has acted in such a way that he has forced the move, he needs help in understanding why he is doing this so that he will not repeat the pattern in his next home.

It is important that the child know the real reasons for the move. Remember that the child tends to blame himself for it no matter what its cause. In fact, people who study children have discovered that a child feels responsible even when things occur which he can't control, such as the death of a parent. Even very young children involved in divorce blame themselves for the family breakup. Realizing this, the adults—if they are controlling the move—should reassure the child that he is not responsible for it, if this is in fact true. But if the child is responsible for the move, he should be told. He should know how he has contributed to the problem, and how his behavior affects those around him. Even when the facts of the move are very painful, the child can accept and live with the truth much better than he can deal with his own confused explanations.

When a child is moved, the other children in the family must be prepared for the occurrence and receive reassurance that they will not be "the next to go." Remember that all children fear having to leave home, especially those children who come to live with a family, formally adopted or not. My husband and I adopted our youngest son when he was four; he had lived with us for two years before adoption. But when he was nine a pre-school foster child who had been living with us was returned to her biological family. One noon-hour as he set off for school after lunch, he stopped and came back. We had the following conversation.

He hugged me and said, "I'm glad I'm not getting moved anymore."

"That's right. That's the thing about being adopted. You can't get moved."

"If you're adopted, you can't get moved?"

"That's right. You can't get moved."

"Good!! Bye." And he was off again.

Jeff had heard this before. But another child's moving made him question his status with our family again, and he needed reassurance. We have discovered that children also need reassurance that the child who is leaving will be okay. Sometimes we have been able to stay in touch with pictures or visits for at least a period of time, and this seems to help both our children and the child who has left. Both need continuity.

The adults in the family must also deal with their feelings about this move. Depending on the circumstances, adults may mourn almost as if the child were dead; or they may feel like failures in some way; or they may feel very guilty for some real or imagined part in this move. These feelings must be reckoned with. If you do not sort out your feelings and deal with them honestly, you may make it unnecessarily hard for the child to leave, or interfere with his ability to make a success of his new move. (For a discussion of this problem, see the section on dealing with failure.)

If the child is moving against your wishes, it is difficult to cooperate. You may be inclined to dig in your heels and fight, then take out your anger on the child when you lose. Or you may abruptly withdraw your affection and leave the child feeling you no longer love him. You may make him feel disloyal to you if he tries to be optimistic about moving on. Or you may cut short the transitional period that he spends with you because it's painful for you to anticipate his leaving.

Even if the child appears anxious to go, and the early visits go well, please do not rush the transitional period. Whether it's painful or happy, difficult or easy, change is hard on human beings, and all of you need time to get used to the new arrangements.

Establishing Values Successfully

It is easy for most parents to find an extra bed, to stretch the food budget a little, and to rearrange family schedules to accommodate a new member. It is more difficult to learn to live with a new child who brings to the family a set of values different from theirs. Though it may seem as though this problem arrived with the new member, it actually pervades our entire society. Everyone is very confused about values.

Most people agree that teaching children values is primarily the responsibility of the family. But if you tried to clarify the point by asking, "What values?" or "What do you mean by 'values'?" agreement would break down. People agree even less about how values should be taught, or how you can keep children from adopting the values of the other institutions that control major parts of their lives—especially the school.

Values is a general word which probably means something different to each person who uses it. It may refer to moral behavior, or to what we consider important, or to what we believe. In discussing values with children, it helps to be specific so the child understands exactly what you are talking about.

Because the subject is difficult and personal, we can't reach a general agreement about it. It may be this lack of consensus that makes the school tend to ignore value questions, even though they agree that they are important. Just as biology books used to ignore the once-controversial subject of human conception and birth, modern textbooks avoid strategic questions of right and wrong behavior. At the same time, they tend to teach a least-common-denominator set of values which offend no one, perhaps, but which also give little help to the student struggling to answer important questions. Of course schools deserve credit as well as criticism. Many of them are beginning to struggle with the problem of teaching values, and some teachers have always discussed values in their classroom.

Whether the school assists or not, you must find a way to help your child integrate ethics with what he is learning and experiencing. The child will need your help to deal with the death of a classmate, with exploitative sex, with drugs and alcohol. For example: An instructor in a high school education class will probably explain the facts of anatomy to him, and perhaps describe contraceptive methods. But the instructor will probably not explain how and when the teenager should use his new sexual powers. In fact, the instructor may discourage those "how and when" questions because the answers are controversial. This may leave the teenager thinking that such questions are unimportant compared to the facts which the school has made certain he learns. How can you be prepared to deal with such questions, especially if the child holds certain values different from yours? Following are some suggestions.

We need to be aware of our values. Sometimes people respond explosively to an action or the expression of an idea and afterwards express surprise at their strong reaction. In most instances one of their strong beliefs is threatened—but they are unaware of just how important that belief is to them. We parents are among these people. Sometimes we say we hold one value but behave in a contrary way and confuse children. For instance, we may say people are more important than things, but then belittle a young teenager and label her as clumsy or careless because she broke a dish. We can correct this behavior: methods are currently being developed that can help us define and express our values. The techniques are grouped under the heading "values clarification"; a local library probably can suggest some materials. The better we understand our own values, the better we can teach those values to our children.

We need to be confident of our value system. No person or group can claim to have a perfect ethical system all worked out and applied to every human situation. Furthermore, none of us practices a system perfectly. But we as parents must develop confidence in our beliefs and practices. That does not mean that we arrogantly insist that everyone else believe and act as we do, but rather that we are firmly convinced that our values provide good guidelines for us and our children.

We need to avoid over-individualizing values. Society's moods swing like a pendulum. Social conformity is popular for a few years; then individualism is the rage. During periods of individualism, people say things like, "Don't impose your values on me" or "Maybe that's okay for you, but I'll do it my way." Such individualism can be valuable, but it is sometimes only a thin veil for selfishness. And excessive individualism tears families apart. Of course families must respect individual personalities and self-expression, but they must also strive to agree about values—and sometimes parents need to impose values on their children. Going to school, showing respect for a sister's privacy—these actions may reflect the parents' values more than the child's values, but the child needs to learn and respect their importance.

We need to apply values flexibly. Sometimes parents face a situation and, instead of concentrating on it, worry about the next possible stage. They start asking, "What will I do if. . .?" and "If I give in on this, what if she. . .?" A family is not a court of law; don't let your children insist you set a precedent you must follow. Deal with each individual situation as it arises.

Here are some ideas from experienced parents:

- Some values are more important than others. Getting priorities straight will save a lot of fights.
- Different behaviors can express the same value. Let a child choose his own way to "do the right thing."
- Children accept the values of people who love and respect them—but this is a *gradual* process. Don't expect instant acceptance or obedience.

Take heart: in the long run, most children adopt the values that their parents lived by.

Providing for Family Unity and Individuality

Many families are finding that outside pressures are splitting them into collections of individuals who happen to live in the same house. Different jobs with different hours make family togetherness occasional; distant schools pull children far away from home; government programs treat people like individuals, not family members. Besides all this, the restructured family faces an additional challenge: trying to unite a group of people who were not always together. This is the kind of family I have. Together we have discovered how to make a close community out of our restructured family.

We operate from a shared value base. Try to think about and articulate what your family values. My family and I are Christians, and we expect that description to meaningfully govern the ethics and behavior of all of us. We try to relate values to behavior first in simple ways, then in more complex ways. Togetherness grows out of this shared understanding of what is important. A discussion of loving our neighbors might result in our participation in a block party, or in a family project of filling a small bank as a gift to the hungry. Because we plan and perform these value-related activities together, our closeness is reinforced.

We talk about our family. We don't consider ourselves merely a group of people who happen to be living together; we are a one-of-a-kind family. Our family is not just bigger or smaller than other families, but different because each of us is different from every other person and adds his unique personality to the whole. When a member comes or goes, the whole family changes, and we talk about it.

We pool our resources. Every member of our family is expected to contribute to the resources of the family, and we discuss these contributions. The children know how much is earned, what mother contributes, what their tasks are. Although the children usually keep and control what they earn, we emphasize that if they choose to spend all they have on luxuries, the family will not have as much to spend on necessities and occasional luxuries. If a daughter buys her own school shoes, we may make a point of buying her an extra, more frivolous blouse so that the connection becomes clear. Or we may buy the whole family a special treat with the money she "saved" the family. In addition, my husband and I try to teach our children that we are not the only family members who can satisfy emotional needs. We encourage the younger children to turn to the older ones for a hug and a Band-Aid. And we assure our children that they are a joy and encouragement to us. Each member is recognized as having resources to contribute: time, caring, love, money, and so forth. We want each child to see himself as a productive and valuable member of our family unit.

All of us participate in decision-making. This means that all family members have access to the information they need to participate in making good decisions. For instance, we always make a mutual decision about the family vacation. We gather and share all kinds of information, and ask countless questions. Who wants to go? Where? When? Why? Are there relatives who want us to visit them? How much money is available? How much time? And so on. Naturally parents cannot abruptly "dump" decision-making on unprepared children, but they can gradually teach their children this skill—a learning process that enhances family togetherness.

We have planned ways to emphasize togetherness. We have developed particular rituals for certain activities and occasions. For instance, we always celebrate birthdays with a meal chosen by the birthday person, with a cake baked in a particular tiered pan, and with gifts—wrapped in brown paper bags—from each family member. The family celebration is held in addition to any other party that includes friends. We also have family rituals for holidays and daily family worship—and it's tradition in our house that the family eats meals together as much as possible. You really have to work at this, since the hectic daily schedules of a family tend to frustrate togetherness.

In addition to providing for togetherness, families need to encourage the individual development of each family member. You may think that this goal is easier to reach—but because of your urge to include the new child, you need to guard against swallowing him up. Here are some things to remember about fostering individuality.

Recognize that shared values can be expressed in various ways. For example: In the community in which we live, the high school emphasizes academic studies, and provides little for students who prefer to work with their hands. You might think that a student who does poorly in this kind of school doesn't value education. Yet if this same student can develop a vocational skill at school, he sees the point of going to school and goes regularly. He *does* value education—it's just that he would rather learn how to fix a motor than read a book. Remember this as you work to establish shared values in your family; allow each family member to express his belief in them in his own individual way.

Encourage individual growth by linking individual responsibilities with individual independence. Give your child as much control as possible over choices; encourage his development this way. Try letting your child express himself by the clothes he chooses. When your child is three he can choose his daily outfit from the clothes you have bought him. At eight he might decide which outfit to buy when you shop together. At thirteen he might shop alone with prior verbal guidance from you about his choice (he is to buy school shoes costing up to so many dollars). At sixteen he may be earning money and buying his own clothes, getting money from you only occasionally for special outfits. This sounds like simple, common sense, but many parents don't initiate this progression. Their first graders never choose what they wear to school; their thirteen-year-olds can't shop alone, and are frustratingly careless about taking care of their clothes. In fact, I once knew a high school senior whose mother was still laying out his clothes every night!

Provide for physical privacy. Because a functional family often ends up with one or two more people than its house was designed for, privacy can be a problem. But everyone needs some place he can call his own. If children share a room, be sure that each child can lay claim to part of the closet and certain dresser drawers. Do not open personal mail, and be sure to stay out of drawers which have been labeled "private"—even if you want to put clean clothes away. Like children, parents need physical privacy. I remember clearly thay my mother's purse and my parents' bedroom were off limits unless she granted us special permission to invade them. In our big family, that was about all the privacy my mother had, and she needed it. Don't be afraid to follow her lead and make some private space for yourself.

Minimize competition. Adults have become quite aware of the danger of comparing their children and usually do not make the mistake of comparing their skills and aptitudes. But sometimes they allow their children to compete in subtler ways that discourage individual development. One may think he has to be the top student to make up for the fact that he isn't an excellent athlete like his brother is. Or a younger sister may try to top her older sister by being a better athlete than her sister was a musician. Try to eliminate even this indirect competition. Assure your child that he is loved and wanted for what he is, not what he does.

Occasionally a child will get extra parental attention because he has problems—either legitimate ones or ones developed to capture attention. Although it may not occur to parents at first, the other children in the family may envy the child who is sick a lot, or who needs a lot of help with homework, or who has a handicap of some sort, because of the special attention he gets. The other children might try to compete with this child by copying him; if they do, their individuality will certainly suffer. Try to discourage this copycat syndrome in your family.

Healthy family life demands both unity and individuality. Balancing them in the functional family requires a little extra attention and skill, but it's well worth the effort.

Handling Fighting and Rivalry among Children

Something which frequently discourages parents in a functional family (and in biological families, too) is the frequency with which their children fight and yell at each other. Not only is it hard on the peace of the family, but it makes the parents wonder how much the children actually love and care for each other. Although all families fight sometimes, destructive quarreling among children isn't healthy, and should be discouraged. Begin to assess and control quarreling in your family with three basic facts in mind.

1. *Remember that the way a child learns to behave with other family members* does *set the pattern for the way he will act with schoolmates, employers, and perhaps eventually with his own family.*

Bad patterns can be corrected later in life, but it's easier to correct them before they're well-established. In addition, a lot of quarreling makes the atmosphere of a home unpleasant. Mealtimes, bedtimes, and other periods when the family should be enjoying each other may become times the parents especially dread. Of course, not all family fighting is bad; it can be constructive. Among other things it can teach a child how to handle conflicts away from home. Solving disagreements, learning to "fight fair," making up after a quarrel—it helps if the child learns these skills in a supportive environment under the supervision of adults who care about him.

2. *Remember that* all *children fight.* Your tolerance for fighting probably depends somewhat on how much your family fought when you were growing up. Of course, two parents may have very different backgrounds. The wife may come from a family in which verbal teasing was allowed but physical fighting was forbidden. The husband's family may have outlawed name-calling but allowed an occasional fist-fight. Obviously this couple will need to compromise to develop a policy for "fair fighting" in their family. You will need to work out similar compromises in your family. As you do so, recognize and respect the unique vulnerability of each member of the family.

3. *Remember that how much children quarrel is greatly af-fected by the age difference between them.* Consider how much quarreling might erupt between a touchy thirteen-year-old girl and a teasing seventeen-year-old boy. Or between a noisy, braggy, ten-year-old boy and a quiet twelve-year-old girl. The general rule is that children less than three years apart and pre-school children tend to fight more. Some experts suggest that parents space their children at least three years apart to avoid the back-to-back problem, though this doesn't always work. Children close in age do get along better in large families than they do in small ones—perhaps because a child has other family members to turn to if he is upset with a particular one.

Following are some suggestions—made according to age group—for minimizing fighting and rivalry.

With pre-school children:

1. *Be very firm about enforcing the limits you have agreed upon*

in your family. Don't let the child hit himself, which he may want to do if he wants to hit someone else but knows he is not allowed to. Avoid being rough with the child, too. Restrain him gently but firmly, removing him physically from the combat zone. Reassure the child that he is good, but firmly insist that you will not allow him to do what he is trying to do. Cuddle him a little as soon as he will permit it.

2. *Don't let a little child hit an older child.* Sometimes we excuse it by saying, "He's just a baby and doesn't know any better." But if rational behavior governed fighting we would have no war. Handle fights by dealing with the emotions involved, not just the reason.

3. *Give the older child private time with you every day, especially if he seems hostile toward a new child or new baby.* Be sure you are not distracted during this time, especially not by his rival. Frequency is important: one-half hour set aside every day would benefit him more than a half-day set aside once a week. During this time, treat him like you used to before the new child arrived.

4. *Get the child interested in some activities outside the house.* You may be able to arrange for him to spend a few hours every week at a play school. Some mothers pool their children and take turns watching them as they play. This doesn't take money and can work very well. Or perhaps you can arrange for a teenager to come to your home regularly—every day, if possible—and play with your older child for a short time. Because the child can't keep track of occasional visits at this age, make sure the visits occur often, though they don't need to be lengthy.

5. *Try to teach your children how to play together peacefully.* Though they may be barely able to do this at first, they will gradually develop this ability if you take time to guide them and make the experience pleasant. Be sure to end these play periods before the children get bored or start fighting.

With middle-years children: Asking yourself the following questions might help.

1. *Are your children quarreling to compete for your attention?* Try to see each of your children as individuals, and spend time talking with each one about the things he enjoys. Don't let

your own interests interfere: remember how easy it is to spend more time with your young athlete than your book-worm if you like sports better than reading. This kind of lop-sided attention can trigger jealous fights.

2. *Do you unconsciously or subtly favor one child?* If you do, the other children may gang up on that child to even the score. You may favor a child because he reminds you of a brother or sister you favored as a child. On the other hand, a child can remind you of a rival from your childhood, and you may be playing out an old battle by siding against him. We do not necessarily outgrow our childhood feelings, and when we're adults they can surface in disguise to plague our family rela-tionships. You may want to ask someone you trust and who knows your family well to tell you if he thinks you are show-ing favoritism, but this is risky if you don't really want to know the truth.

3. *Is one child quite cleverly disguising his provoking behavior to get you embroiled in the fight?* This trick won't work well if you make it a rule to stay out of your children's fights. Don't try to judge who is guiltiest, who started it, etc. Separate the children, but don't hold a trial.

4. *Is the fighting just a habit?* Occasionally family counse-lors work with a married couple who seem to be what they call "conflict habituated." That is, they fight all of the time, they don't seem to want to stop the fighting, and it apparently bothers other people more than it does them. If your chil-dren's fighting is a habit, take steps to break it as you would any other bad habit your children might have developed.

5. *Are you making too much of "fairness"?* School-age chil-dren often put their parents on the spot with the accusation, "It's not fair!" Parents sometimes encourage this rebuttal without meaning to. With good intentions they divide each candy bar equally, they purchase equivalent gifts on special occasions, they carefully remember whose turn it is to take his bath first, or to help hold the dustpan. But instead of convinc-ing the children of their fairness, the parents just succeed in focusing their children's attention on justice by measure-ment, and the children begin to examine every situation for the merest hint of unfairness. It is better to let children experience a little inequality, to explain that it isn't practical to

always expect things to be exactly equal. Naturally I am not saying that one child should always be the one to be shortchanged, or that you should purposely cheat a child in some way because "that's the way the world is and he has to get used to it." I'm simply saying that exaggerated attention to fairness may increase rather than diminish the normal rivalry between children.

With teenagers: Realize that teenagers should handle disputes like adults—or at least be learning how to do so. They will do more screaming and door-slamming (or whatever is acceptable as a way of showing emotion in your house) than you would like, but if you have handled earlier fights as suggested, they will be learning to handle conflict the way you do. Of course, in a restructured family a newly added teenager may not be familiar with your way of handling arguments, or he may be copying the destructive fighting patterns of the adults in his old home. Whatever your circumstances, the suggestions below might help you.

1. *Be sure your teenager knows the ground rules in your family.* In our house we have, among others, these rules: No name-calling is allowed. Words like "stupid" and "pig," racial epithets, and so forth are banned. (It has been popular lately to say that such terms are "only words," to point out that children themselves often use the rhyme, "Sticks and stones may break my bones, but words will never hurt me." But this rhyme developed because children *do* believe there is harm in words, and believe that rhymes of denial will help ward it off.) We also prohibit profanity. Generalizing is also considered unfair in a fight, because it is too hard to deal with. We ask family members to stick to the specific problem and avoid vague accusations like "You never help me" and "You're always picking on me." We also outlaw physical fighting.

2. *Expect the teenager to respect your family.* We expect our teenagers to show family loyalty and respect family privacy. Most teenagers have at least one friend they can count on to keep a secret, and they sometimes confide in them about family problems. But we generally encourage our children to consider family fights family matters to be settled internally. It is not considered fair in our family to publicize the weak-

nesses or disagreeable acts of a particular member.

3. *Avoid playing referee when teenagers fight.* We give our teenagers opportunity to settle their own conflicts. Try not to interfere when your teenagers quarrel unless they are seriously breaking the family rules about fair fighting.

4. *Be sure the children know that they can come to you for help if they cannot figure out how to settle a fight. Do not act as judge.* Show them some techniques for constructively settling fights, suggest a compromise, or in some other way offer a solution, but do not impose it if you can possibly avoid doing so. Instead, have them make another attempt to solve the problem for themselves. Imposed solutions almost always result in another fight later, because one child or the other is sure to feel cheated by the adult's decision.

Raising the Child of Another Race or Culture

After a period of hoping and working for an integrated society, we are in a period in which we are thoughtfully re-evaluating what we have accomplished. This re-evaluation has particularly affected attitudes toward cross-racial placement of children in families. What about the child—black, Indian, Korean—who is raised by a white family? How is he affected—not only as a child, but as an adult—when the society he lives in probably will still be marred by racism. The response to the evaluation has ranged from "I don't see any problem" to "No child should ever be placed in a racially different family." If you are raising someone else's biological child who has a different ethnic background, you probably have some ideas on the subject yourself. You might agree with the latter statement, but you might be raising a child who has been with you awhile whom you love and want to "see through." Or perhaps you sincerely believe that you can make this child's life with you a good experience for him now and good preparation for his adult life.

The following section largely explores the views of parents who are raising children racially different from themselves, and the ideas of psychiatrists, psychologists, and social workers who are especially concerned with this issue. I urge you to seek out other sources, too. Much good literature has been written on the subject. Read some of it, apply it to your own situation with common sense, and go on raising your child with confidence.

Raising a minority child in a white society is different, but not all parents want to accept this fact. I understand this; as a foster parent I myself have often rebelled mentally at the insistence that any foster child is somehow "different." "But," I would say to myself, "he's just like any other child—he has the needs and wants and hopes of any other child, and my job is to do the best I can to meet them." Certainly there is a sense in which this is true. But I have also had to recognize that a fundamental difference *does* exist: unlike most children, this child has been separated from his mother and father. With that fact comes a bundle of "stuff" which must be dealt with in parenting him. And a minority child brings with him an additional bundle of "stuff" that must be contended with. It does not go away because we choose to believe it doesn't exist or doesn't matter.

To parent these children, we must also accept the fact that we need skills we do not have. Most minority parents have automatically taught their children the things they need to know to survive in a white society—things that most white parents aren't aware of. One of the worries of welfare workers helping minority children has been that white parents simply do not know how to give the minority child the psychological defenses and skills he needs in a "white world" to maintain a positive feeling about himself and stay emotionally healthy. I believe white parents can learn these skills, but only if we listen to those people—minority parents, among others—who understand them and can articulate them.

Now let's consider more specifically three factors important in raising a minority child in a white family.

Most important is the child's self-image. A healthy self-image is fundamental for any child, and is based on the same foundation in all children—on a sense of belonging, a sense of competence, a sense of worth, and a sense of meaning. So what we would do to develop a white child's self-image we can also do, appropriately, to develop the minority child's self-image. The black or Indian or Vietnamese child can believe that he is beautiful and worthwhile because he belongs to one of these races, and that is O.K. But even better, I think, is the child's believing first that he is a beautiful person *apart* from his racial identity—that becomes the secondary way he identifies himself, not the primary way. If he doesn't like his personal identity, he will have a hard time valuing his racial identity, whatever that may be.

In a way, though, personal identity can never be separated from racial identify—a fact that makes people especially concerned about the minority child being raised by white parents. Let me illustrate this self-image problem by considering what it means to effectively parent a fat child in our society, in which being fat invites criticism and rejection. Researchers have found that a fat child has much more difficulty maintaining a positive self-image. Coming at him from all directions are a hundred different messages which suggest that to be fat is bad. His classmates believe, among other things, that fat children are lazy, and that fat children are more likely to cheat. He is likely to be the last child chosen for the team, not just when athletic skill is required but even when it makes no difference at all. The fat child has two basic ways to cope with this situation: he can resolve to lose weight, or he can say to himself, "I choose to be fat." Of course, he can also deny his fatness or insist that it doesn't bother him, but these tactics will not help him build a positive self-image. A caring parent will try to help him in a couple of ways. He will reassure the child that his body build is okay because it is a part of him— like his eyes and his sense of humor. He will also encourage the child to diet or exercise to make physical changes that *he* wants—not ones that other people want.

Like fat people, people of minority groups are often spurned by our society. The parents raising such children must realize that they receive hundreds of negative messages about their racial identity. A fat child can change his build, but the minority child cannot change his race, so he needs help to avoid denial or rationalization of one kind or another. He will need this kind of reassurance: "To be dark-skinned and have kinky hair is okay because you're okay. If you want to wear your hair in an Afro, that's fine. But if you choose some other style because you like it—not to copy someone else or to try to deny that you are black and have kinky hair—that's okay, too."

A second responsibility of the parent is to help the child develop a strong racial identity. Sometimes minority children do not identify themselves as different. You may ask, "What's wrong with that?" Not necessarily anything. Most of us feel that racial sensitivity and prejudice is learned, and that socially innocent children are refreshingly interested in their *likeness* to each other. But sooner or later the child will be confronted by the fact of racism. He will be called "nigger" or "chink" in a belittling way, or he will become aware of much more subtle things like being left out of birthday parties taking place at certain private homes.

If a child is unaware of racism, he may develop two serious problems. First, he has to assume that there is something wrong with him personally that causes people to respond negatively to him. Second, he has no adequate defenses that permit him to continue thinking of himself as a worthwhile person despite the negative messages. Even assuming that you live in a community which accepts minority children (and none do totally), your child will grow up to live in a world that will often judge him and discriminate against him on the basis of his superficial racial characteristics. If you lovingly help him accept and appreciate his "difference," he will be less vulnerable to the prejudice he faces outside your home, and more able to cope with racial bigotry as an adult.

So far I have talked about racial identity as if it were only negative. This certainly isn't true. Besides preparing your child to handle the problems of his racial identity, you have the opportunity to make him aware of its joys. Give your child opportunities to study the history of his race, to learn about his culture, to value its heroes. Do culturally enriching things together: read stories, watch TV specials, and go to plays and movies produced by or about other races, especially his own. He also needs opportunities to get to know other people of his race from all social classes, in all kinds of occupations. This is an ambitious undertaking, so get help with it. Your child's school should be willing to help, both because it will be good for your child and because it will be valuable for the "majority" children, too.

A parent has a third important duty to his minority child.

If you are teaching him to be aware of injustice and to work to
make life better for all people, he probably will want to become involved in the fight for civil rights and racial equality. It
is the responsibility of those raising children to make them
aware of the way change is brought about, and to help them
develop effective skills for participating in groups. Your active
participation in organizations will provide a good model. We
have plenty of people who are good at pointing out problems
and complaining about wrongs; teach your child to be one of
those who not only see the problem but also help solve it. Give
money to the causes you believe are important and encourage
your child to do the same. Go to the trouble of finding ways to
let him participate—stuffing envelopes for the local fund
drive or walking in a local "Hunger Hike." Talk about the
goals, methods, and successes of various group organizations. Point out their limitations and failures so that your
child has a realistic idea of what can be accomplished. If he is
idealistic, he may become frustrated and angry if he is not prepared for occasional failure. And always be on guard against
having your child used to advance someone's personal
interest in the name of cause.

Besides the long-term goals of raising a minority child, a
parent faces challenging questions about day-to-day living. Let's
consider some of those.

The first question might be, How do I help my child be proud
of himself and able to defend his identity without making him
hypersensitive, hostile, and overly aggressive? When a racially
aware child looks around him at the world in which he lives, he
may very properly respond by being angry. But anger takes
energy—energy needed for constructive activities. And a child
will often turn his anger against those he loves, not against the
problem itself. He needs to learn how to channel the energy from
this anger into positive actions. As he does this, he also needs to
learn what to ignore, what to challenge, and how to accomplish
the most with the least effort. Here are a couple of examples.

Recently I was walking home with a neighbor's child and
heard a child in a nearby group call "nigger" in her direction. Both
the child and I pretended not to hear it—not, I think, the worst
reaction. But now that I've done more reading about blacks and
racism, I think it would have been better to say, "That kid must

really have problems if he has to call a pretty kid like you names."
That would have prevented an embarrassing confrontation for
the girl, yet let her know that she was okay and that the other
child's epithet was his problem. A good second step to take would
be to identify the name-calling child and talk to him and, possibly,
his parents, because I believe adults should make clear to their
children that such behavior is unacceptable.

Here's another similar situation: a high school girl of mixed
race was finding racist notes left in and around her school locker.
An older black student made it his business to find out who was
writing the notes and gave the information to the guidance
counselor, a sensitive and capable person. She talked to all of the
boys involved, warning them that more severe action would
follow if there were further incidents, and put a stop to the
behavior in that way. The young man could have offered to beat
up each boy he caught writing the notes, and the situation could
then have escalated into a major incident which used up a lot of
energy and goodwill and accomplished little. But the student
chose to react in a positive, dignified way, helping to solve the
problem with concern and yet a minimum amount of energy.
Like him, your child has other things to accomplish besides
fighting racism, though that is extremely important. Try to
help him keep a sense of proportion and work for change in
constructive, economical ways.

Although you want your child to learn how to cope with
racial slurs, you don't want him to get the idea that every negative
remark made to him is inspired by racism. All children get criti-
cized sometimes just because adults around them are having a
bad day, and they are convenient targets. And all children set
themselves up for criticism by misbehaving occasionally.
Remember this when your child tells you about some supposedly
racist incident; be sure you get the facts before you begin fighting
for justice. He may be trying to find out what you would do "if"
this were true, or trying to distract you from some misbehavior
of his own. Keep in mind that race is only one part of your child's
relationship with others. You will do him a disservice if you permit him to hide behind his racial identity. Don't let him say, "I got
a 'D' because my teacher doesn't like Indians" when you know he
hasn't been studying. And don't let him use certain injustices and
disadvantages as excuses to resist the opportunities he does have.

Remind him that members of minority races will probably have to provide the bulk of the initiative and drive to win full justice for themselves, so he has a responsibility to develop his potential, not ignore it.

The older minority child may get caught up in expressing his racial identity by certain behaviors which are supposedly "black" or "Indian" or "Mexican." These are similar to every older child's attempts to belong to a peer group by wearing similar clothes and having a similar hairstyle. A child's choice of ethnic music or hairstyles or similar things is fine so long as he doesn't feel he has to choose these things in order to be *really* black or *really* Indian. Your child will also discover the symbols and symbolic gestures of his race. You will want to read about them so that you can help your child understand their meaning and value. This is a highly controversial matter—something your child should realize. Of course he should express his ethnic identity, but never in an offensive way. If it's bad manners to wear a hat in buildings in your community, your child should remove his hat even if wearing it is ethnically significant to him; he should find an inoffensive way to express himself. It helps if you and your child are both good-willed and willing to compromise—valuable traits whenever parent and child together shape a child's personal habits and beliefs.

The child you are raising may also be hurt if members of his race question his identification with that race because he is being reared in a white home, or because he doesn't have to endure the poverty which is often the lot of minority children, or because he has tastes or interests which don't fit the racial stereotype. It will help if he has regular contact with adults and children from his racial group and many opportunities to explore and develop his own racial consciousness. If he is secure in his personal identity, he will not be easily threatened by those who challenge his right to belong where he chooses. He should realize that he has the right to develop his potential, follow his tastes, and capitalize on the resources available to him, so long as what he is doing does not hurt someone else, or infringe on another's rights. No child should be trapped in a racial stereotype, either by society in general or by the minority group to which he belongs.

What if your child never comes to notice his racial difference or make comments on racial issues? This situation is similar to the one in which an usually curious child doesn't ask questions about sex. A child is aware of racial differences by age four or five, and if he doesn't mention them he has gotten a message that the subject is taboo: you can avoid this problem by giving the child natural opportunities to talk about his being different. When he is four, you could mention that his pretty brown skin is different from yours. This would give him the freedom to "notice" the difference. Or you might try a more general approach, as I suggested in the chapter about acknowledging absent parents. Use a TV news story or a picture in the paper to bring up the subject. Bud don't overwhelm him with it. Once you have made it clear that racial questions and problems are open for discussion, he will discuss them. Of course, the ease of your discussion will be affected by your basic confidence in and frankness with each other, and by the child's age—the older he is, the more challenging the discussion might be.

CHAPTER 6

FOR PARENTS ONLY

Meeting Your Own Needs

Rearing children—your biological own or someone else's—is the most interesting and challenging task in the world. Motherhood has been my profession for almost twenty-five years, and I have found it calls for all of the dedication, skill, intelligence, and hard work which makes the life of any other professional useful and satisfying. It is a good life's work; for me it has been a full-time job.

This does not mean that I consider child-rearing my whole life, nor that I think parent-child relationships are primary in a family. Strong families develop out of strong marriages; the most important relationship in your home is the one between husband and wife. Especially in a functional family, the danger is that the needs of the children may overwhelm the marriage. One or both parents may purposely put the children first, thus undermining the marriage. Or the sheer amount of time and energy invested in the children may leave little time for privacy and little energy to work at the marital relationship. In the long run, both marriage and children will suffer from this neglect of the husband and wife for each other. This book is not about marriage, but much has been written to help adults build good marriages. I urge you to read relevant books or consult a minister or counselor if your marriage is not what you hoped it would be, or isn't moving toward that goal.

Adults need to set aside time for themselves. Time used to develop your own life is not time stolen from the family. It is essential to your well-being that you invest time in enriching yourself spiritually, emotionally, intellectually, and physically. And some of what you do should be directed toward interests other than child-rearing. A worker who invests all of his energy in his job becomes a dull person, and very often his work eventually suffers as well. When he retires, he dreads the free time that other retirees welcome: he is cut off from the working world that obsessed him, and has no outside interests or hobbies. To a greater or lesser degree, parents retire too when their children become adults—a transition you must plan for carefully. Much as you love them, don't let your children crowd out your other important interests.

Getting Help with Parenting

You may be a parent who is unhappy about your present situation as a parent. One of the following statements may express your feelings about your family and your personal life.

"When I married Jim he was a widower and his two boys lived with their grandmother in another state. Now they're living with us. I know it sounds ridiculous now, but when I figured out what becoming a wife would mean in my life, I never really thought about what it would be like to become a mother to his kids. I don't feel very good at it and, frankly, I don't like it much."

"Jeff and I worked very hard to get him through school and support our two babies at the same time. We really looked forward to the time when I could stay home and he could work. Now I'm home, and his kid brother has come to live with us, too. I'm doing what I want to do and what I think I should do, and Jeff is just tremendously supportive, but I feel so alone and out of it professionally. I get so tired of having people look at me as though I'm wasting my life because I'm not working as a nurse anymore."

"I'm just plain tired. Sue and I both work because it seems like we just can't pay the bills for five kids on my teacher's salary alone. I try to help with the kids and the housework, but we never have time for each other anymore, and I'm getting so I fly off the handle at our second boy almost every day. A couple of days ago I hit him a lot harder than I meant to, and it scared me."

"I'm a nag. It's funny. Only it's not. My mother used

to nag me all the time, so I vowed I'd never be like her. But here I am, and I can see Judy just turning me off like I did my mother. I'm still not close to my mom, and I'm scared I'm losing out with Judy, but I can't seem to stop myself."

"Sometimes I have such an attack of self-pity I feel like I want to go to bed and stay there forever. I didn't ask for this kind of a life, and I feel like I'm getting gypped. When we adopted these kids we did it together. Now Pete has walked out, and I'm stuck with all the work and all the struggles. What can I do? Is just surviving all there is to life?

"I like being a parent—most of the time I enjoy the kids. But I'm really scared when I think about trying to deal with them as they get older. I really feel like I haven't had much preparation for being a parent, and I wish I knew how to handle things better instead of just muddling through and patching things up afterwards."

"I have really tried—the whole family has tried. But Jane just doesn't want to fit in with us, and things are going from bad to worse. I admit I wish we had never said we would take her."

If one of these speakers sounds like you, if you are in a situation which leaves you feeling dissatisfied, helpless, or alone, you *can* change things. Even the most hopeless-looking situation can be improved substantially: families that are just getting by can become strong, united, happy groups. But it will take work and a willingness to change. Are you unhappy enough to struggle for change?

One of the best things you can do for yourself is seek out a group of parents who are experiencing similar problems and doing something about them, and get some help from them. You may not realize how many of these groups there are, or how valuable they can be to you. Let me describe some that are currently available in my community. Look around your community; you can probably find similar ones there, or find someone to help you start the kind of group you need.

Child Study Groups (Also called Parent Education Groups). Under various types of school and community sponsorship, these groups emphasize educating parents about children. Parents get information about the needs and characteristics of children, ways of managing behavior, and techniques for improving communication and problem-solving. In the process the parents get to know one another and give each other friendship and support.

Parents Adopting Children. Frequently sponsored by adoption agencies, these groups provide adoptive parents with support, encouragement, and information during the transitional months or years before and after the child joins the family. Often these groups also try to meet the needs of children awaiting adoption, to educate the public about adoption, and to work for legislation to improve adoptive procedures.

Family Living Groups. These groups—often sponsored by churches—try to involve both parents in the program, and deal with husband-wife relationships as well as parent-child relationships. They emphasize the importance of the family's spiritual life. Besides providing helpful information, the group is structured so that families work together to achieve their goals.

Foster Care Associations. Often chapters of state or national organizations, these groups are made up of foster parents and social work professionals involved in the formal foster care system. They emphasize mutual support, provide education about the characteristics and needs of foster children, and advocate public and legislative action for foster children.

Parents Anonymous. These groups are fairly new, created for parents who are actual or potential child abusers. In these groups parents help each other discover why they are having trouble coping with their children and how they can better manage their problems. Very important is the support and solicitude the parents provide each other. If you think that you might be hurting your child in any way (by verbal abuse, physical punishment, or emotional withdrawal),

Parents Anonymous urges you to join them.

Parent and Child Groups. Usually focused on the pre-school child, these programs are designed to help the parent and the child together. Leaders are available to observe and help with parent-child interactions. The groups discuss topics of concern to parents, but the children are always present, and the setting emphasizes learning primarily by doing, not by talking. In my community this group seems to be attractive to young professionals who are taking time out to stay home with their children and are interested in doing a good job. At the same time, they help each other to grow personally, in "non-parental" ways.

Parents Without Partners. This group has three basic goals: educating parents to handle the special problems and needs of single-parent families; providing mutual support for single parents; and providing a social life for single parents and their children.

How to find the groups you need. Because communities vary so much across the nation, it is not easy to tell you exactly how to get in touch with a local group that would be the counterpart of some I have described. Most of these groups are staffed by volunteers; sometimes the group name changes; often funds are limited and the group can't afford to publicize itself. Because of these fluctuating factors, it might be a challenge to find telephone listings for these groups—but keep trying. First check a variety of possible listings. And keep in mind that the telephone directory for some communities includes a section in the early pages with a title something like "Human Services Directory." Scan this list for the names of groups or agencies that deal with your area of interest. If you call one of them, someone there may be able to give you the name of a local contact.

If you can't find a phone number this way, try calling your pastor, phoning the "Y," contacting a Family Service Agency, or checking with the local crisis center, which often maintains a list of all sorts of community groups. If one group doesn't seem to fit your needs, try another. And if you can't find a local branch of the organization you're interested in, remember that you can probably find other people who are interested in forming a local chapter or group.

• Marriage Improvement Groups. One of the best is Marriage Encounter. Contact local pastors, or write Worldwide Marriage Encounter, 3711 Long Beach Blvd., Suite 204, Long Beach, CA 90807.

• Child Study Groups. Call your local community college, child guidance center, or school counselor. Family Service of America may sponsor a local group or know how to get in touch with one. F.S.A. will be listed in your local telephone directory; you can write them at 44 E. 23rd St., New York 10010.

• Parents Adopting Children. There are several national organizations and many local groups. Contact the local adoption agency or write to one of the national organizations for names of local contacts. OURS, Inc. publishes a newspaper and has local chapters; it is particularly helpful with special needs and international adoptions. You can write for a membership brochure from the main office, located at 4711 30th Ave. S., Minneapolis, MN 55406. You might also want to contact the North American Council on Adoptable Children, NACAC Resource and Membership Office, 3900 Market St., Suite 247, Riverside, CA 92501. It publishes a newsletter and works for improved legislation; it particularly supports permanent situations for children.

• Foster Care Associations. The only national organization devoted wholly to foster care is National Foster Parents Association, Inc., P.O. Box 257, King George, VA 22485. There are state and local chapters, and local foster care groups, but not all are known by or affiliated with the national association. Call your local foster care agency, probably located in the Child Welfare or Social Services office.

• Parents Anonymous. National address: 22330 Hawthorne, Suite 208, Torrance, CA 90505. Call the local Child Abuse Prevention number or the Crisis Center for the name of a local contact.

• Parents Without Partners. Since they are often sponsored by a local church, call a downtown church office or the local ministerial society. Our local group meets in—of all places—the Volunteer Fire Department Hall. You may need to be persistent to locate this one.

Living in families is not easy; no family finds it smooth sailing all of the time. Raising someone else's biological child poses special challenges, because usually it means learning to love a stranger. Adults who have long ago given up the "love at first sight" myth in adult relationships sometimes are disappointed that it takes so long to develop a close relationship with their new child. Occasionally a parent tells me that the closeness he longed for between himself and his child never developed.

It is very risky for us to expect love to govern our relationships: we cannot take love for granted or wait for love to happen. Perhaps it is better if we make our goal mutual respect and tenderness. We do not have to feel love to show kindness, consideration, accommodation, and consistency. If we do show such concern, I am convinced that strong feelings will follow. With this in mind, treat your child as you would if the loving feelings were there. Give freely without asking that the child return all that you give. Love won't develop overnight, but it may grow gradually. In fact, many parents raising other people's biological children have eventually developed a close and loving relationship with their child. This love is all the more precious because it is not a response to a biological debt; it is a free response to your special care and concern.